YOUR PURPOSE IS
YOUR PLATFORM

YOUR PURPOSE IS YOUR PLATFORM

reaching the next level

Jeremy Perry

Foreword by: Armica Nabaa

© 2018 Jeremy Perry
Believer's Breed, Inc.
P.O. Box 291
Mount Juliet, TN 37122

All Rights Reserved. No part of this book may be reproduced, stored in a retrieval system, or transmitted by any means without the written permission of the author.

For information about special discounts for bulk purchases, please visit jpbelieves.com.

Photo Credit: Shutterstock by permission

ISBN-13: 9780692047590
ISBN-10: 069204759X

Printed in the United States of America

Dedication

This book is dedicated to my mother and father, Mr. and Mrs. Tyrus Perry. I would like to thank you for the warm, constant embrace of affirmation and the countless moments of laughter. Both of you have been so influential in my pursuit of purpose. I pray this book is a near perfect reflection of the passion you have helped me discover. I look forward to where life's journey will take me next. Wherever it takes me, I know you two will be there to provide continued support. Love you forever.

Table of Contents

Dedication · v
Foreword · ix
Introduction · xi

1 **The Inspiration** · 1
2 **Stretching** · 20
3 **Dream Team** · 36
4 **Servant Leadership** · 52
5 **Weight Lifting** · 70
6 **Momentum Swing** · 86
7 **The Moment You Have Waited For** · · · · · · · · · · · · 98

Foreword

I often come across ambitious, talented athletes, but even in our first encounter, there was something extremely special about Jeremy. With today's pressure to conform to societal standards, Jeremy has dedicated his life to helping people find their purpose and embrace their individuality. His meek, giving spirit exemplifies that of a true leader doing God's work and living out his own unique purpose. <u>Your Purpose is Your Platform</u> is a reflection of Jeremy following the direction of God to empower people to fulfill the capacity of their potential. Jeremy has taken his engaging teaching style to philanthropic efforts with his organization and now to the world as an author. This book teaches practical, powerful principles that can help guide anyone to living out their true purpose. Jeremy takes his experiences in the world of athletics and provides informative metaphors that provide insight to anyone looking to reach the next level. Jeremy's leadership is truly inspirational, stretches you to greatness, and inspires you to bless the world with your gifts.

Armica Nabaa

CEO, ATB Management Group, Inc.

Introduction

Most of us can feel a fire burning inside that screams for us to live a productive life. That fire makes it clear that we are put on earth for a reason. There's a point in life when we search for that unique platform to open doors for our prosperity, allowing us to live a fulfilled life. Searching for this platform is often a grueling process because we have overcomplicated the ideology of success. Although our world is always evolving, it is important that we equip ourselves with core values that remain consistent. This book is a plea to find your inspiration and allow it to saturate you to the point of overflow. There is no need to live your life in circles by attempting to be someone you were not destined nor designed to be. We all have gifts that we should use as our benevolent offering to the world. However, to truly understand how to reproduce success, it is important to grasp the practices that lay at its core. Everyone has a wealth of experiences that mold their innermost being and create metaphors that draw parallels to life. For me, many of those experiences came from a life submerged in sports. This book uses these metaphors as motivation for you to find your voice in a world with so many people silenced by their circumstances.

A world with people utilizing their purpose to its full capacity is a world that will blow our minds and redefine the boundaries of our platform.

We are all uniquely designed with innate gifts that are an essential part of our identity. It is so amazing to know that we are all uniquely designed to travel various paths. There are so many thoughts that enter our mind daily and many of them are focused on finding our purpose. My hope is that this book will encourage you to find that purpose and establish core values for repeated success.

1

The Inspiration

The definition of success has been tainted for quite some time in modern day culture due to the attention granted to those that live elaborate lifestyles and often create a spectacle each time they appear in the public's eye. Many of us are bombarded with overwhelming exposure to the misconception of instant gratification. The watered-down notion of overnight success has become the focal point of many people's journey to find their purpose. As generations pass, there is a movement further and further away from the true essence of sacrifice, diligence and accomplishment. For me, this movement became evident within the world of athletics. Throwing balls, making diving catches, and sprinting past others are only a few highlights that often become attached to athletes at a very young age. More often than not, many of the eye-catching feats began as innate gifts and these gifts blossom to set many kids apart in a world of their own. This special breed of athletes sharpened their gifts over time to fit the mold of some competitive sport that has been encouraged by the awaiting world around them. Everyone does not possess the genetic makeup that sets him or her apart as an athlete; however, everyone possesses a gift that is designed to benefit others. So many people make the fundamental mistake of searching for their platform without first searching for their purpose. In my adulthood, I find myself learning many of life's best lessons from kids. As I peered to the front of my church one Easter Sunday, I saw how several kids anxiously battled with one another for the microphone to recite the speech they had been practicing for weeks. After being calmed by supervising adults, the young boy who fought most aggressively for the microphone emerged to center-stage first. After gazing in the eyes of the awaiting audience, he was frozen with nothing to say. Even at a young; innocent age, he fell into the fundamental trap of pursuing his platform without first pursuing his purpose. For us, this flaw doesn't manifest when fighting to give an Easter speech, but it has affected us all at some point in our lives. It's such a dangerous mistake to seek recognition and popularity as an assessment for success. Just because there is a stage doesn't mean you have to stand on it. Life will present many opportunities to emerge onto a platform that does not coincide with your purpose. These opportunities will leave you feeling empty and dissatisfied. There's no such thing as finding your platform. Living in purpose creates your platform.

Oftentimes we are pushed to expose our superficial gifts because they are popular or 'cool.' Take a moment to think about it. Have you suppressed your true purpose because it wasn't what you would consider a grand assignment? You may have concluded your purpose wouldn't place you on televisions across the world or make you a household name. So, like many, you decided to chase something that would. This neglect of your true reality can be connected to Sigmund Freud's age-old superego component of his psychoanalytic theory. The superego is manifested as a form of moral righteousness created by those external factors of one's being that include parents, family, coaches, friends, etc. If not properly assessed, upholding the moral standards created by these external factors creates friction with the internal reality of a person's heart. Therefore, it is vital to seek true *inspiration* opposed to molding to external influence. This journey is difficult because affirmation from others around grows to become an instrumental part of our happiness.

Finding true inspiration starts with suppressing the expectations of others in order to create a clear canvas for your passions. Leonardo Da Vinci didn't paint the Mona Lisa with brushstrokes from Pablo Picasso or Andy Warhol, but he occupied the canvas with brushstrokes, ideas, and inspirations from his own soul. The fortitude created by inspiration pushes you beyond the need for affirmation and will tear down the apprehensive barriers of uncertainty. During the pursuit of your platform, it is vital to gain more than a sense of the "status quo" inspiration. Regarding abstract phenomena, like inspiration, society's standards place limitations in order to derive a basis for explanation. When people can't explain you, or fit you into their own selfish mold, it frustrates them. Therefore, defying those limitations can cause friction with others around you. It should be woven into your daily journey to find not what inspires you, but your inspiration. You may ask, what's the difference between inspiration and being inspired? Glad you asked because this chapter is dedicated to setting the foundation for the difference between the two.

 What or who inspires anyone can be changed or taken away within moments. There are 1.8 human deaths per second. Therefore, allowing people to serve as your inspiration may not be your best bet. Without a doubt, some will dare to say the death of loved ones serves as their inspiration. I will be the first to say that some loved ones that I have lost inspire me daily. Nonetheless, when thinking of the moments I had with these loved ones, I never remember them telling me to make them a monumental figure in my life to look up to once they made their exit from their physical body. However, the summation of lingering thoughts from my life's pioneers reminds me to find my own purpose and embrace it. Look at it like this. Think for a moment about someone you inspire. If you could script your last conversation with this person, what is it that you would say? What message would you want to leave with them for eternity? Would you say "tattoo me on your arm as an inspiration to live the life I led?" Or maybe you would say, "Every morning you wake up I want you to dwell on my legacy so you can follow my footsteps." That conversation can be much more productive. If I had the luxury of scripting my last conversation with a person whom I inspire, I would not leave the selfish request of following in my footsteps behind to anyone. Naturally, we love and will forever cherish those family and friends. We also hope to leave behind a favorable legacy, but I would rather people pave over my footsteps to create their own. Your loved ones fulfilled their own lives and now you must complete your journey with no regrets in order to fulfill your own destiny.

Additionally, I haven't felt the urge to make someone who is still living my inspiration. The water that floats someone else's boat is likely to sink yours. Yoking inspiration with someone living can be more dangerous than pairing it with someone who is deceased because they still have the breath to change from day to day. An example can be having a best friend as inspiration. One day your best friend may smile from ear to ear in contentment while mentally walking through a field of sunflowers. The next day that same friend may be crying in disappointment while mentally lying in a valley of darkness. Inspiration is not characterized by this inconsistency. Inspiration comes from the deepest caves of the heart, and will not falter from day to day. Inspirational passion will remain lit. It doesn't have a face. It doesn't have a name. There is no dollar amount. This is all because true inspiration lives and feeds on itself, and has no need for external nourishment or refill.

In my lifetime, I have had dozens of interviews that span from recapping my college experience to job opportunities with multi-million dollar corporations, but one interview still stands out because of its correlation to this inspiration we are all seeking to find. After the general manager at one particular Logan's Roadhouse in Nashville asked me questions during my interview, he gave me the unique opportunity to ask him questions. My last question to him was, "what are your expectations of me?" Before answering this, there was no possible way that he could know how his answer would paste itself on the beams of my memory. He gave me a list of practical things that he expected, followed by a less detailed list of more intellectual related expectations. He covered the basis for what my role would be as a team member in the restaurant and how customer service outweighed any other policy in our handbook. That portion of the answer was rather predictable. However, to conclude his answer, he stated, "You will never live up to my expectations. You can ask anyone around here, I'm never satisfied." That latter portion of his answer revealed to me the incapability we possess in upholding the expectations of others.

Regardless of how much you strive and strain to meet someone else's expectations, there will always remain the continuous paradigm of dissatisfaction.

As Lebron James hoped to meet the expectations of his new Heat fans during the 2010-2011 season, he finished second in the NBA in scoring, averaging 26.7 points per game. He also led his new team to the NBA finals where they fell short to the Dallas Mavericks. After losing this series, the criticism of James skyrocketed to unbelievable heights for arguably the best player of his era. Aside from the individual accolades, it was not enough for James to lead his Heat to an eleven-win improvement upon his arrival. It wasn't until James escorted the Heat to win the NBA championship the following year that he received a few ounces of respect. Although this 2012 championship season was coupled with James winning both the regular season and Finals Most Valuable Player, he still fell short of expectations. He then became the cynical focus of comparisons to other greats like Michael Jordan and Kobe Bryant, both having multiple championship rings to boast. If James' inspiration to play basketball was measured by the satisfaction or happiness of his fans, his career would have ended long before its maturation ever began.

Money is a subject that brings some people to tears and others to smiles in the same setting. Some people crave it and others save it. Some people were born into financial circumstances that allow them exposure to vast resources and the ability to create generational opportunities. Others struggle to establish financial stability and simply are attempting to survive. American Society leads the way when it comes to being inspired by money. From the most minuscule foundations of education, children have become consumed by a false sense of platform. The platform in the minds of many youth involves a great degree of wealth. As a result, an overwhelming majority of Americans view wealth as their platform to reach their destiny. In all reality, your purpose is your platform. The very reason of your existence gives you complete access to the real estate that your platform will reward you with. In other words, your purpose opens the door to your destiny. By no means should obtaining wealth be frowned upon. I strongly encourage everyone to reach a place of financial stability that creates opportunity for generations of the future. However, don't let the bulk of your existence be controlled by the most influential piece of paper ever known to man, the dollar bill. Being motivated by money symbolically reveals the pains, the tears, and the obstacles in your life have bounties. Maybe you feel money is your inspiration. Take a moment to think about that. People frequently ask what happens when that money is gone? Others ask about where the wealthiest of people allocate their money. I believe those concerns should be a tad bit different. The questions that burn the outskirts of my heart are connected to the person and not to the dollar. What happens when money no longer inspires you to get up early in the morning to get better at your craft? Which dead president do you talk to when tears soak your pillow from disappointment? How do you continue to impress after people have seen your top-of-the-line home and car?

This is the reason that people and things may very well serve to inspire you to attain certain goals within your lifetime, but inspiration allows you to wake up happy every morning despite your acquisitions or shortcomings. Inspire is an action word (verb). However, inspiration is a noun that denotes a deeper connotation that refers to the life of the word. Adding the suffix *"tion"* transforms the word from a verb to a noun. In doing so, this word goes from a verb that is dependent on an orchestrator to a noun that can exist within itself. Take for example the word *"reveal"*. As a verb, it is up to something or someone to reveal whatever it is that they have the secret to. Translating the word from *reveal* to *revelation* gives it life beyond the control of the orchestrator. A revelation can stand alone without being put into motion by someone in charge. Another example can be made of the word *"tempt."* This word is inexistent and irrelevant without a tempter due to the word being a verb that must be set into motion. However, the noun *"temptation"* is present with or without someone to set it into motion. A teenager might be tempted by his friends in a gas station to steal some alcohol. The friends serve as the tempters that set the thought into motion. On the contrary, the presence of *temptation* to steal alcohol can enter the mind of this same teenager even if his or her friends were not present. *Temptation* becomes life and has its own existence based on its origin and nature. Instead of friends being present to *"tempt"* (inspire), *"temptation"* (inspiration) now becomes the lifeblood that prompts actions. This is the basis behind finding inspiration! Inspiration has its own origin and nature that is nearly resistant to all forms of configuration.

To be inspired is a temporary feeling that is emotionally driven by moments in time. Former NFL center and older brother of Cam Newton, Cecil Newton, once shared with me some chilling stories about Ray Lewis. As Lewis' former teammate, Cecil once told me about how Ray was able to render inspiring pregame speeches that gave his teammates a rush of emotion that seemingly gave them a superhero state of mind within that moment. I'm willing to argue that despite how passionately Ray Lewis gave his pregame speeches, he could not inspire anyone that couldn't draw from a wellspring of inspiration that they already possessed. The heart cannot separate itself from true inspiration, but the two have a relationship with the intimacy as a mother giving birth to her child. Similar to a mother finding out she is pregnant; when someone finds inspiration, there is a sense of joy and expectation about the future. As an infant develops in their mother's womb, the development of someone growing in route with their inspiration brings pains. The biggest pain often derives from seeing the vision of the future while juggling the struggles of growth towards that promise. Now for the contractions! The closer you get to experiencing inspiration bolstering you into your vision, the more the pains whisper in your ear to give up. Finally, when the struggles subside, you can birth your impact to a world starving for your presence.

Some people never face doubt or uncertainty when discovering their inspiration, but most do. Understanding inspiration can be difficult if you're looking through the wrong lens. So often, people analyze their future as if they are looking into a mirror. When looking into a mirror, you see yourself. When looking into a mirror, your vision is selfishly aimed at your reflection. This perspective gives us more of ourselves without any ability to change the image that is reciprocated off the glass of the mirror. It is this concept that is stapled in the mind of people from the earliest years of acclimating to life. To this day, my mind is drowned with echoes of countless motivational quotes from nearly every coach I had. One that continues to crash into the rocks of my memory is, "take a look in the mirror." Quoting this always took place when our team was down with the hopes of finding rejuvenation that would carry us to a victory. Of course, I know what my coaches were trying to say.

They wanted each of us to take a deep look within ourselves to find that foundation we could anchor to in times of distress. However, in hindsight, I find this to be one of the most selfish requests that a person can make. For when we all truly look in the mirror on our journey to our desired future, it produces a self-centered blueprint that will seek to satisfy our pride opposed to our purpose. Much differently, looking through a lens allows you to see an image of what's before you with the ability to focus the lens to give you an image that is bigger and more concise! Digging even deeper with this revelation, one of the main constructs of a telescope is a warped mirror. So instead of looking into a selfish mere image of a future revolving around ourselves, we should take the time to morph our perceptions into a focused alley of purpose. Gazing through the focused lens of a telescope has allowed us, earthlings, to see images of planets, moons, and other amazing forms of creation. Though these images are miles upon miles away from our vantage point, we can see them once the lens is focused. This is the ideal perception that should be taken towards looking at your future. Though goals and visions may be discouragingly distant from sight at the moment, having the right lens perspective can allow these distant claims to be brought into focus for a clear picture. Perhaps coaches should reconsider their heroic comeback speech to incorporate a lens instead of a mirror. Opposed to players looking into a mirror of themselves, they can look into their team's lens to focus on what may be a distant goal. Although distant, with the right vision it can be brought into the reality of attainment.

By shifting the focus of life to the greater good of the world, the vision of inspiration will draw near to the heart. This only happens because here is when the motives become selfless, and you realize what piece you are to the world's incomplete puzzle. As a kid, putting together a puzzle was a challenging, yet exhilarating experience. All is well until one piece seems to keep eluding you. There's just an uneasy feeling of pieces being out of place. As a result, you can't experience the joy that comes along with feeling complete. In terms of well-being, the world as we know it could experience exponential growth if everyone realized what piece they were to the puzzle. A puzzle piece can only possess an inkling of significance within itself because its value is enriched when it becomes a part of the collective entity known as the puzzle. When selfishly searching for your inspiration, you will become disappointed at the continuous feelings of empty vanity. During the pursuit of my M.A.Ed. degree, my graduate assistant supervisor was Karon Fairs. The first day I showed up to work she tossed me a handful of keys to open the door to the office where I would be working. She didn't tell me which key I needed to use to open my door. As with many cases of trial and error, there were a few errors. None of the keys worked in my attempt in opening the door until I got to the last one! Each time I stuck a key in the lock, it felt like it was the match. Needless to say, I was denied access when attempting to unlock the door. The same concept lies behind finding true inspiration. People often possess a number of innate gifts or convictions. Operating in a facet of your gifts or endowments may feel right for only a moment's time. You may find yourself happy one day feeling like you have found your life's match. Then you realize you are wrong. The next time you are wrong. The next time you are denied access. You then find yourself feeling defeated with little hope of reconciliation to the ambition you possessed at the beginning of your quest for inspiration. I advise you to search until you find the key to unlocking your life's treasures. Nobody will have to tell you that you have found your inspiration. There's no denying this gut feeling! If you are searching for your inspiration and purpose, be sure to give yourself the opportunity to find it. This information age we live in doesn't offer much peace and quiet. That serenity is what you need to discover the gifts that were placed inside of you. Reward yourself with the decency to hear from your own heart. The chaotic sounds of television, radio, and cell phones can drown the quiet rhythm of your heartbeat. Take some time to be alone and discover that purpose that lives in you. Once you discover your inspiration, you will experience the peace of fulfillment for a short time. Soon after, get ready for a war within!

As you begin to take the focus of your future aspirations off yourself by allowing your inner realities to take precedence, you will begin to feel a sense of connection to your inspiration. When you become connected to inspiration, you become disconnected to areas of your life that are unfitting to your purpose. At this point, you may realize that your inspiration is not answering your boss's phone calls or working in the heat of a factory. You may realize your inspiration is not tied to becoming a medical doctor or a politician. For most people, this juncture of life is confusing and frustrating because of the friction surrounding this evolution. This is the point when you struggle to step outside of your comfort zone into your purpose. I will cover more on this comfort zone in Chapter 2. When I began feeling my inspiration tug at my heart, I wrestled day and night with feelings of falling out of love with football. My earliest recollections of playing football date back to the dusty fields of Hillcrest High School in Memphis, Tennessee. This is where my father began his coaching career. I quickly found that I loved tossing the funny-shaped brown ball into the palms of the sky to descend into the arms of those teenagers my father coached. It wasn't long before I started to hear emphatic comments about what people felt was an impressive arm I had.

From there, I began playing organized football at age nine. I got my start at playing quarterback after throwing the ball back to my coach after running a routine route as a wide receiver. My competitive nature kicked in during my middle school years as we played games against friends we grew up with in our neighborhood. I discovered in high school that I was in love with football and wanted to play forever. Earning all-state honors was just icing on the cake for me. My goal was never to receive accolades, but I was simply showing football the love I felt it was showing me. Football rewarded me with being able to play in college as a two-year starter at Tennessee State University. Surprisingly the latter part of my loving relationship with football was characterized by feelings of doubt and uncertainty that was catalyzed after losing my starting role my senior year. Like many athletes at this cliff of apprehension, I questioned if I still loved the game. I did and still do! Your inspiration may not be tied directly to something that you have grown in love with from your childhood. This does not reflect a lack of love, but only says that your inspiration is in a different place.

In 2010, I realized my inspiration did not lie between the lines of paint on the football field. My mother and father inspired me every time I played a game, but they were not my inspiration. My heart goes out to everyone that supported me, but they are not my inspiration. I definitely appreciate every coach that taught me, but they are not my inspiration. Each of these instrumental people inspired me on a daily basis. However, they were not the "noun" inspiration. They all showed me how much I really did love peering through the facemask on my helmet to stare into a boisterous crowd of sixty thousand fans. I will never forget looking into the eyes of a teammate after he straps his shoulder pads on for what seemed to be his preparation for entering a battlefield of World War III. The taste of victory is still so sweet and I will never lose that competitive drive it takes to be a champion. However, as my inspiration started showing its face, I realized that winning games were only an appetizer for my life's entrée of service.

The calluses of holding on to the dreams that others have for you are helpful in letting their dreams go in order to pick up your own. In your life, you should reach a point when you are doing something all day without the worries of compensation or gestures of affirmation. Then you wake up the next day to do the same thing. If you are looking for handclaps of approval or pats on the back, change what you are doing. The praise of people should only be a side effect of your platform. Again, your purpose is not about you! Whenever you reach the plateau where you want to pull others into your peace and that peninsula where you are surrounded by contentment, you have found your inspiration. When paying you cents less than nothing gives you the same joy as becoming a millionaire for operating in your purpose, you have found your inspiration. Nobody has to tell you to work hard. You will never lack enthusiasm. Most importantly, people operating in their inspiration will always take a backseat to selfish ambitions to arrive at a selfless satisfaction.

REFLECTION POINTS

Imagine this: Envision yourself living a life focused on your purpose instead of your pride.

Answer this: What is your inspiration each day you wake up?

Try this: Refocus your vision to see how your purpose benefits others opposed to yourself.

2

Stretching

The process described in Chapter 1 is the most difficult part of any journey. The foundation, that takes root at the humble beginnings, often poses the most strenuous labor en route to the creation of a valuable byproduct. This ranges from building homes to creating businesses, and even as you learned-finding inspiration! The foundation is the most taxing part of the journey because it is driven by internal battles that cause you to develop the intrapersonal relationship with yourself. If you keyed in on the nuggets to finding true inspiration in Chapter 1, hopefully you noticed that every detail dealt with self. The biggest obstacle for anyone stepping into the competition of life is the fear that their dedication will not reimburse them worthily. That's a battle with self. The disruptive thought of not making your family proud is a battle with self. Deeming your true value to the world is a battle with self. The Beatles were first denied a record deal because their sound didn't appeal to certain record labels. Because of their self-ambitions to follow their inspiration to create music for the masses, they are arguably the best band to ever grace the soil of the earth. Even now, tunes from many of their records uphold their legacy. When Michael Jordan was cut from his high school varsity basketball team as a sophomore, he had to deal with thoughts of doubt, disappointment, and desire. Jordan wasn't cut completely from participating in basketball, but he was assigned to the Junior Varsity team. His decision to keep pursuing his dream by using his shortcoming as fuel was a battle with self. To disconnect yourself from the expectations of others in order to grab hold of your inspiration is a battle with self. Fighting those domestic battles inside your head and heart sets the scene for you to begin grabbing life by the horns. This is where your interpersonal victories give rise to let the world see your light shine!

There is such irony between the complexities of mankind and their routines. On one hand, we have the ability to create, analyze, and solve life's most intricate matters. Human ingenuity has opened the door for endless possibilities. On average, we make approximately 35,000 decisions per day. The capacity to ration such a hefty part of our mind to make decisions is impressive in itself. In addition to decision making, we are gifted creators. What my grandparents considered a great figment of the imagination has become reality in so many ways. For them, it was a seemingly irrational thought to think that a car could operate without a driver. Thanks to the brilliant minds of the automotive and engineering industry, we are now being driven by cars. The thought of accessing thousands of articles at the click of a button could only be dreamt about. Thanks to Google, the library is now located wherever your heart desires. The thought of a phone being portable was a stretch. We now live in a culture where most kids have never seen a landline phone and are able to pay for groceries with a cell phone. It is such a staggering thought to realize technology is literally taking over our world. Despite our continuous development and growth on so many levels, there are some things we dare to change. As a means to remain plugged into our fast-paced society, we humans become routine as we matriculate through life. The alarm clock sets the day in motion for most people and the routine that is unique to every individual tends to remain the same for a great portion of their lifespan. It's the monotonous cycles of everyday living that often cause us to miss out on what we are to truly enjoy with our gift of life. In most homes, the alarm clock initiates the beginning of days as a signal to prepare for the journey that lies ahead for the next few hours. For some, the alarm clock interrupts the peaceful unconsciousness of sleep. For others, the alarm clock signifies a new day with new opportunities. What causes people to view the beginning of the day differently from the next person? Some people despise their daily routine and others cherish it. It seems that I hear conversations on a daily basis about strategies to living a life of fulfillment. There is something important to note after you find your inspiration. Simply finding your inspiration is only the beginning, so now it's time to begin the process of unfolding your purpose. If you plan on running the race of your life, I advise you to stretch properly.

Everyone makes claims that they want to be in charge of their destiny. On most occasions, I believe that people would really like to take charge of their life, but the reality is, most people do not know how to begin taking action. Just as world-class sprinters stretch before running full speed, we must learn to master that important concept for ourselves. It is so vital that you begin by *stretching* outside of your social and cultural comforts. The American society is arguably the most self-centered maze of all macro-communities in the world. Our culture's self-centered disposition has made front-facing cameras a norm for phone manufacturers. As if that weren't selfish enough, we have even submerged the phrase "selfie" into our daily lingo. At one point, it was weird and somewhat cynical to see a person taking photos of themselves. Now our homes, social media, and phones are unapologetically flooded with self-taken photos. Having accountability for your neighbor is farfetched in America due to the selfish, capitalistic drywall behind the foundation of the country. As a result, we often forego expanding our horizons beyond the perimeters of people identical to ourselves. Fear of changing the routine that has become the identity of American life is a very crippling barrier on the path of progression. Your purpose is dynamic. The word *dynamic* stems from the Greek word *'dunamis.'* The original definition refers to the inherent power that a person puts forth. Your purpose has power. However, that power is to come forth and be experienced by others. As I began to expand my horizons by questioning those both inside and outside of my race, creed, and culture, I realized that the perceptions of most people are the ones given to them by their parents, family, and teachers. The everlasting question of 'why' became the centerpiece of my focus when conversing with others on a daily basis. To my surprise, there was rarely solid rationale for people's ways of thinking. This is when I realized the futility of the average person's answers to simple questions about certain goals, beliefs, and perceptions were due to the lack of exposure. Too often, we take what we learn from others at face value. It's either us being naïve or lazy. The truth awaits those who seek it. Asking the question 'why' has given me prized insight to paths that others fear treading. During the first phase of my career in education, I observed several of my college mentees over the span of an 8-week semester. I quickly became intrigued with the level of commitment from one of my students. Chima Azuonwu came to me from Delta State, Nigeria and possessed a passion for academic growth that I had never witnessed. Most students I mentored were typical college students with a desire to graduate and create an opportunity for themselves in the workforce. Chima's desires spread well beyond simply wanting to graduate and enter the job hunt. As you can imagine, with little time spent in the U.S. before entering college, his English dialect was strangled by his thick Nigerian accent. He sat with me for hours at a time reading sentences aloud in an effort to grasp the English language. Chima held reading material about an inch away from his face as he followed along with his index finger to track word by word. When he was unsure of a word or its pronunciation, he would pause to look up at me for guidance. Time and time again, he stopped me mid-sentence to inquire about the meaning of a word I previously uttered. At times, I was unsure if I was making any progress with helping him become acclimated as a college student in America. When writing papers for his freshman English courses, it took Chima hours to construct a seemingly simple paragraph. Many days, I left the office scrambling for more ideas on how to ensure his ability to handle the rigor of college academics. When I presumed he was tired and frustrated, he would walk through my door again. The tenacity with which he approached his education was unmatched and I knew there had to be a driving force behind his determination. One day, after we wrapped up a session, the forever looming question of 'why' would not let me remain in the dark on why Chima was so adamant about his education. I looked him in the eye and asked, "Why do you care so much?" I followed with comparisons to his peers and pointed out that his zeal was not typical amongst his colleagues. Because I asked this question, my eyes were opened to Chima's world. He made it clear that a college education for him was not simply the next step to take after graduating from high school. However, in Nigeria he was raised under the ideals that a college education in America was a privilege that would afford him opportunities to make large-scale impact both in America and in his home country. He went on to tell me more about the political ramifications that hindered educational opportunities in his home of Nigeria. Stretching outside of my social comfort allowed Chima and I to build a bond that became rooted much deeper than learning to pronounce different words of the English language. It allowed me access to the place of his inspiration and gave me an appreciative perspective to build upon.

Destroying the yokes of an ignorant mind begins with *recognition of self-worth*. Recognizing the value that you add to the big puzzle discussed in the previous chapter gives you insight to the reality that others also possess something that is unique to them. You begin to grow curious as to how others fit into that puzzle. I'm so grateful for the memory God has granted me. I can remember details from events that occurred in early stages of my childhood. When we sit and reflect, my mother is often shocked with how vividly I can recall certain memories. Sometimes it is the description of clothing or maybe even a visit from a family member. There are details that grab my attention and seem to never let go. I don't have to rewind time as much to recall an exciting visit to the fingerprinting office. I was on the brink of landing my first job and this was the final stage of the application process. As the generous attendant rolled each of my fingertips on the detection pad, I could see my print on the computer screen in front of me. The magnification given by the size of the computer screen allowed me to see the sophisticated patterns for each of my fingerprints. I never knew each print encompassed such great detail. I paused for a moment to embrace what was actually happening. I went into the office simply to complete the last task of my job application, but I left with much more revelation. That was me on that computer screen! Those fingerprints I saw are exclusive to me. There are over 7-billion people on this earth, and to know that we are so matchlessly unique is eye-opening. Why should we crowd each other's purpose? You have worth! You have your own distinct purpose! Even identical twins have different fingerprints. We are all distinct individuals at our core. That's the beauty of life. I once called one of my closest friends to ask if he believed in me. He responded, "yes man, I truly do." I told him I was appreciative of his thoughts of me. I also told him that his answer didn't have any bearings on how I felt about myself. Subsequently, whether he believes in me or not, I know my worth. Never question the magnitude of your existence. There are already enough people to doubt your worth; don't you join their team. Self-worth is not predicated on the thoughts of others about you. It is the intrinsic value that you possess just by being you. There are not any qualifiers for self-worth, and there is not an evaluative measurement tool that can legitimize or diminish your worth. It should give you such joy to know that your worth is not tied to your performance. Even better, it is comforting to know that your worth is not tied to your lack of performance! However, your worth is tied to your purpose. The mark you make on the world is going to have your exclusive fingerprint.

As you begin to grow out of your shell of sheltered teaching, you grow into the *recognition of false pretense.* This part of *stretching* involves revitalization through the creation of real emotions based on true perceptions that are created from the depths of our inner selves. This will bring you an excitement that is stirred up from the soul because you are finally shedding skin that has covered up the true you for so long! No longer will you regurgitate the words given to you by your mother. You will no longer view the world through your grandfather's eyes. The storied past of your coach will not be the underpinning of your perceptions anymore. By no means is this an overnight process. Your mindset will not be altered in a matter of seconds. It takes time to undo the misconceptions that have been developed. I don't want you to believe that people in your life were steering you in the wrong direction or seeking to sabotage your views on the world around you. In fact, many of the lessons we learn from our circle of influencers should be powerful and applicable when moving towards your purpose. Yet, based on our experiences and maturity, all of us are limited in our perception. Many of the pretenses we are taught are developed from a lineage of people who never asked the question 'why'. Some of the greatest turmoil between various ethnic groups has lingered from generation to generation with no true lines of communication to identify the true matters and causes of conflict. I once witnessed the aftermath of an altercation that involved three men. Two of the men were brothers and recently had a physical altercation with the third gentleman. Evidently, the fight began with one man vs one brother but escalated as the other brother walked onto the scene shortly after the squabble started. In his questioning regarding the incident, the police officer asked the older brother why he joined the fight opposed to help peacefully resolve the conflict. It was concluded that he had no idea why his brother was fighting, to begin with. This is the same unwarranted conflict that is carried on between people of different beliefs, backgrounds, and identities. Too often we join ideological and theoretical conflict on the simple merit that those closest to us have taken on those unjustifiable biases. Can you provide logical justification for your perspectives? Hold yourself accountable to discern your own false pretenses. Ridding yourself of these biases will open your eyes to some cool stuff! This change will slowly guide you into the *recognition of beautiful diversity.*

    The beauty of diversity smacked me in the face when I realized that music from other cultures made me dance. I found myself enjoying some amazing Caribbean tunes while celebrating my younger brother's college graduation. These sounds from the islands were refreshing and new to me. That was some of the best partying in my life! I also realized I enjoyed John Mayer just as much as John Legend. I could jam to Maroon 5 the same way I jammed to the Jackson 5. As much as I enjoy the soulful sound of Faith Evans, I'm equally infatuated with the catchy vibe of Faith Hill's "Mississippi Girl." Remaining completely honest, there is some music that I will never enjoy. That preference differentiation extends to art, clothing, and every other element that defines diversity. Yes, some things will be distasteful to you. When we have the willingness to be vulnerable to diversity, we are all entitled to distaste and dissatisfaction. The fact of the matter is we must open ourselves to stretching outside of our comfort zone long enough to develop empathetic perspective. Pulling muscles is the result of athletes not stretching before going forth with physical activity. The outcome of an athlete pulling muscles is stagnation when seeking to move forward in the process of reaching their potential. We should ponder on this with our lives as well. Stretching into unfamiliar territory should be uncomfortable. Stretching should produce some awkward moments between you and others. That's okay. Appreciation for others awaits on the other side of those awkward moments. Not stretching to what may be discomforting at times causes us limitations in moving forward in the race of life. If you haven't, I encourage you to explore various horizons. Try some new foods. Go some new places. You may not learn a new language, but grasp a few phrases in a language other than your own. Legendary coach Phil Jackson said, "Always keep an open mind and a compassionate heart." This philosophy manifested itself through Jackson's eleven successful championship teams during his coaching career. His most noteworthy Chicago Bulls teams were characterized by the willingness for each player to maximize the team's success by playing their role. How do you personally attest to the difficulties that come along with trying to galvanize a group that is comprised of individual agendas that exclude the priorities of the team? For Phil Jackson, it was the Bulls, but for you, it may be family. It may be your employees. Maybe you are struggling to build on the unity of your organization. Stretching looks different for us all, but the benefits are common. Gifts and talents without a supporting cast are as useless as jet skis in the desert. Having this openness that Phil Jackson referred to will thrust you into the true essence of life and creation, unity! Carbon dioxide teams up with water and sunlight to create oxygen that we need to breathe every second of the day. The moment we inhale that oxygen and exhale it back out as carbon dioxide, the process repeats itself. The heart pumps blood to our brain in order for the brain to orchestrate the body's functions. This process happens continually without us having any regard to this precious working relationship. Uniquely, both of these processes involve elements of nature working together for a goal that benefits the whole.

Maturity births understanding. Understanding brings about willingness. Willingness is the bridge that allows you to cross the threshold of uncertainty, apprehension, and fear. Looking past social and cultural barriers, that make us each unique, will allow you to gain an outlook on life that is not concerned with race, background, religion, or any other stigmatic dividers that have plagued us. Opportunities are missed, relationships are forgone, and controversy is sparked because of our unwillingness to *stretch* outside of our selfish comfort zones that were created from our conception. Some of the greatest relationships are built when two people look past the glaring differences in their lives to see the hidden similarities. Sometimes we are so intently concerned with how we differ from the next person that we overlook the common ground on which we both stand. After all, you have nothing to lose by taking time to explore different cultures, lifestyles, and beliefs. The worst that could happen is that you despise the differences in others, and you return to the way of life you're accustomed to. The best that could happen is yet to be known because there is immense upside to uprooting the weeds of a barricaded mind. Take the time to stretch as you begin running with your vision.

REFLECTION POINTS

Imagine this: Envision a world without negative racial, cultural, and systematic barriers.

Answer this: What are three ways you can create a new outlook on your purpose?

Try this: Empower yourself daily to learn something about a culture aside from your own.

3

Dream Team

One of the most impactful lessons I learned at an early age came from my mother. Even now, I hear her stern voice reminding me, "choose your friends wisely son." We do not understand these types of lessons until we grow older and begin to embrace wisdom and maturity. Thankfully, I lived long enough to understand the importance of what she told me. Filtering my friends was not always a simple task for me because I saw something positive in every friendship I had. I still battle with this concept, because I'm so highly engaged with empowering people. As a kid, my life revolved around athletics. Most of the friendships I formed were with my teammates. These were the boys I spent the most time with outside of home and we formed a contagious habit of winning. As we grow older, we are exposed to more. More people. More information. More decision-making. Friendships began to grow more complex. It was often hard to distinguish the right time to create intimate bonds like that of the teammates I grew up with. However, there is no greater teacher than experience! I learned that people formed friendships for different reasons. Some people wanted friends for influence, while others were concerned with gaining access. There were also those that wanted friends in order to feel protected. That was when childhood began to lose its innocence, and I quickly began to understand what my mother meant by choosing my friends wisely. Everyone has memories of their first discomforts with ending friendships that were not beneficial to personal growth. Even as adults, many people struggle with severing relationships that have proven to be more of a burden than a benefit. It often takes us coming to *'the last straw'* moments before we end contaminated relationships. Sadly, it is often too late because of the damage already done. It's time to wise up and start inspecting our relationships on the front-end. This will save you from a bunch of headaches down the road. The concept of filtering how you chose to build connections covers the spectrum of all relationships. From intimate relationships between lovers to the bonds created with peers on the job, it is extremely important to practice wisdom when picking those you allow to share your efforts, time, and space. Taking a stand to remove yourself from unhealthy relationships will give you a greater sense of your purpose.

There is a wise saying that quotes, "birds of a feather flock together." This statement could not be any truer! In 1992, some of the best players in the NBA linked up to become what we know today as the *"Dream Team"*. This team of NBA superstars was formed due to the disappointing third-place finish turned in by the 1988 Olympic team in Seoul, South Korea. Up until this pioneering moment in NBA history, the Olympic team was an assembly of college players who didn't have professional playing experience. As a result of the embarrassment in 1988, Earvin "Magic" Johnson, Larry Bird, Michael Jordan, and other great players decided they would come together to show every nation that the United States was home to the best basketball players in the world. More importantly, they set out to prove they could assemble a team that would mesh beyond differences of background, experience, social status, or other culprits of division. When I was of age to really understand this gesture that took place in 1992, I was amazed at the essence of what happened. The 1988 Olympic team was characterized by youthful, unseasoned college players who were unaware of the vision of their teammates. These players had no intentions on sharing the stardom they gained as collegiate players. There was not a single player on this team who had reached age 24 by the 1988 Olympics. This young, vibrant group simply enjoyed the opportunity to play in the Olympics while wearing a Team U.S.A. jersey with their name stitched on the back. Four years later, there was a remarkable transformation of perception with the 1992 team. This team was characterized by savvy, proven veterans that shared the same vision as their teammates. Their intentions were to erase the doubts that surrounded the superiority of United States basketball. By unparalleled margins, they drove that point home to the world and left Barcelona with gold medals dangling around their necks. Michael Jordan said, "Talent wins games, but teamwork and intelligence win championships." The toughest competition this team faced was practicing against each other. The players were not overly concerned with playing games against other nations. They practiced with such intensity against their own teammates that the games came easy. A crucial junction of our success is that we surround ourselves with people who will push us to be our best. We need people in our lives who stand with us before the glitz and glamour. Selfless determination to accomplish a common goal is the fundamental nature of teamwork. In order to remain progressive, it is imperative that you pick yourself a *Dream Team*. The winning edge for the 1992 Dream Team was the ability for individuals to recognize their own strengths and weaknesses. Being open to self-critique allows for the people around you to help minimize those weak areas while maximizing your strengths. This is vital to the stability of your platform and the fulfillment of your purpose.

The most valuable friend in the world is one who values a friend. An eagle that spends all day around chickens will never fly. The eagle will vainly possess the ability to fly while limiting itself to the terrestrial life of a chicken. Learning to fly is a side effect of determination and a byproduct of vision. The combination of the two reveals dissatisfaction with current status and the fortitude to make change. That word 'vision' is often misused to describe sight. Sight is simply seeing yourself and others in the present state. However, vision is being able to see yourself and others in the future. Being stuck in the present will place limitations on people's ability to be progressive. Enjoying the present is very important. In fact, I wear a wristband each day that says, "Win Today." Each day presents battles and it's your obligation to attempt winning them all. The moments of excitement and happiness that accompany enjoying the present are priceless. It's important to slow down and enjoy the beautiful moments we are blessed with each day. However, having vision allows you to remain focused on your desired future despite the obstacles or stumbling blocks that may infiltrate your path daily. The next statement could easily be the most important part of this entire book. Purpose leads to vision. Vision leads to your platform. You need people around you that understand vision and how it gives you confidence that your purpose has impact. Keep friends that have vision because they see past your potential, and they actually envision you in the future. This ideology will create friendships that motivate individuals to push their friends from their present, past their potential, and into their future. Potential energy has no value if it never becomes kinetic energy that takes action. Unfortunately, too many people go to the grave holding on to potential. Is there a person whom you consider to be your friend that has never hurt your feelings with criticism? If so, you should reevaluate that companionship. Dream Team friends don't mind hurting your feelings in order to preserve your purpose. The moment a baby eagle sees another eagle in flight, it realizes the capability it possesses. At this point, the baby eagle has an inner fire that will no longer allow it to be satisfied in a nest. Just as humans, the eagle has doubts that develop from lack of experience. It is then when the eagle's mother pushes it from the nest and forces that apprehensive eagle to utilize its flying capabilities. Imagine if that eagle was never pushed out of the nest and forced into flight. Don't live life from the nest. The world has so much to offer. More importantly, you have so much to offer to the world. Being surrounded by people who recognize the potential you possess is very advantageous, especially when doubt creeps into your mind and prevents you from taking the faithful step into soaring from potential to purpose.

When you are assembling your *Dream Team*, one of the most important players to pick is your mentor. Plato and Aristotle had Socrates. Gandhi had Dadabhai Naoroji. Jordan had Phil Jackson. Success breeds success. Mentoring relationships involve a developmental foundation with a more experienced person providing guidance and advice to a less knowledgeable or less experienced individual. This developmental relationship allows people to be nourished by someone that has fought some of the same battles and endured many of the same struggles. Mentoring takes place on various levels, but the motive should always remain the same. Growth! This is a symbiotic relationship that fulfills both individuals on a progressive basis. The Princeton University Press defines symbiosis as "when individuals from different species form persistent associations in which they all benefit." Mentors should not shun the notion of tough love. The guidance from a mentor should always be in the best interest of the mentee. For this reason, it is important that you choose mentors who are not afraid to tell you the truth. Merriam-Webster defines truth as "the property of being in accord with fact or reality." Dreams and endeavors often become saturated with opinions and biases based on selfishness or ignorance. Simply not knowing factual truth and having substantial evidence of reality can hinder you from tailoring your vision into proper perspective. We often become so wrapped up in our dreams that we lose a sense of reality. Having a good mentor to serve you up a dose of truth is a tremendous asset. Mentors are not designed to destroy your unconventional dreams, but rather to polish your vision and blueprint accurate steps needed to make those dreams a reality. Dream big. Think big. Believe big. Big goals must be accompanied with an unparalleled work ethic that puts you in position to excel. Mentoring relationships are not one-sided, but mentees should take full advantage of the opportunity to exhaust their mentor as a resource. Mentees should be drowning their mentors with questions, seeking advice, and constantly bringing ideas to the table. Questions are the highway to knowledge. During many conversations, I provide a disclaimer about my binge for asking questions. This usually prompts others to ask questions, and before you know it, questions are bouncing back and forth in conversation. I've discovered that when asking questions, I usually leave with more knowledge than I intended to receive. That's such a fulfilling moment! According to Forbes, the number one tip in regards to mentor-mentee relationships is to "regularly schedule meetings with your mentor and make it a part of your standard workflow." Be a sponge, and soak up every piece of valuable information possible. Mentees are not to be robots that take action based on the command of their mentors. However, they reject passivity and become active in the critique of themselves. The relationship with your mentor is an opportunity to take a reflective look at your strengths and weaknesses. Make meetings productive by pinpointing specific areas for improvement and growth. Don't presume this is a plea to ignore your strengths. In fact, recognizing areas for improvement should be an introspective gauge of your strengths. When speaking to my student-leaders about growth, I encourage them to "peel back the layers." I'm prompting them to dig deeper than the surface and make continuous strides towards the core. On the surface, you may be a great communicator. However, once you peel back that strength layer, you may realize you can improve on the variation of your tone when speaking on diverse matters. For those who are great with relationship advice, how can you peel back the layer to reach the person who has been through multiple divorces? There is always room to make improvements on your strengths. Having a good mentor is vital as you evaluate necessary strategies for making advancements to expand your platform. If you are not mentoring at least one person and being mentored by at least one person, then you have some work to do! Go seek, find, and build these relationships in order to draw closer to your goals, while pushing others closer to their own.

    The other members of your *Dream Team* should include a person with passion, a person with poise, and a person with perseverance. Passion is contagious! The energy given off by passion can give you the spark needed to take the next step. This person with passion needs to be someone who is not afraid to speak to you with authority when you veer from the path of purpose. This person speaks from the heart and gives life to your vision. At times, they may seem more excited about stepping into your purpose than you are. This fire will help to keep you burning through times of discouragement or even boredom. All of us experience those monotonous moments when days seem to lose the thrill of adventure. There are other moments when ideas don't flow as freely as they once did and you struggle with innovation. Pulling ourselves out of these slumps can be tough. In these valleys, your passionate team member can share the much-needed energy to give you a sense of rejuvenation. Sometimes all you need is the feeling of a fresh start. Passion is the addiction that comes with new beginnings. This rush of excitement is infectious and nourishes us with the energy to keep moving forward. Bill Gates once said, "You can't get people excited unless you can get them to see and feel the impact." There will be times when this member of your Dream Team will have to remind you of the impact your purpose has. Knowing that your purpose has impact stirs up the flame living within you. When I speak with teachers who have spent years in education, the common thread of their longevity is seeing impact. Watching the lives of young people develop under their tutelage gives them the excitement to keep pushing. Mary Alice McWilliams was a teacher for more than five decades, most of them being in the Memphis City School System. Her impact has been felt for generations and her legacy continues to flourish through the many students she empowered along the way. She even taught the former Mayor of Memphis, Willie Herenton. Her daughter, Melanie McWilliams Stafford, says, "My mother was passionate about teaching, especially mathematics. Her students were not provided the best resources, and were labeled by society as being 'less than.' For her, teaching math meant more than just teaching formulas and equations, it was teaching them the skills of reasoning and critical thinking to make wise decisions. My mom remained a teacher for over 50 years because she knew the big picture for her students and was excited to help them gain the confidence to overcome the odds." That's passion! We all need people in our lives that help us remain passionate about our purpose. When this person says you need to get more excited, believe them. If you aren't excited about your purpose, you will never reach the platform that awaits you.

The Dream Team member with poise is a healthy balance to the person with passion. Poise is not characterized by a dull, nonchalant personality. However, this person embodies the ability to always remain focused regardless of the chaos that comes with your purpose. When you experience moments of panic, doubt, and disappointment, this person will be right there to assure you that better days will come. Even during the good times this person is there to keep you level-headed and fixated on the vision. Your platform should never take you too high or too low. The rainy days will come in each of our lives, but this person is on your team to make sure you don't drown in sorrows or defeat. It's easy to take umbrellas for granted. They sit idly in our homes, cars, and offices until we need them. Being caught in the rain without an umbrella is frustrating, embarrassing, and can be overwhelming. It's not that the rain can prevent you from reaching your destination; it's only water. However, it can frustrate you to the point of quitting before you get to where you need to go. Getting soaked by the rain leaves you feeling as though you are no longer fit for your destination. You need this person of poise to be an umbrella for you. This is someone who can be there to shield you from the overwhelming, rainy moments in your life. When you are overwhelmed, you don't need everyone around you to be overwhelmed too. In these difficult moments, you need someone to reel you back in and regenerate your sense of stability. Contrary to the dark moments in our lives, we will experience the highlights of life. These are the good times. Business is good. Ideas are flowing freely. Opportunities are on the horizon. During these good times, it's easy to forget about the rainy days. This is when our person of poise is there to help us remain grounded and in pursuit of purpose. This Dream Team member is not to make us dwell on the rainy days, but to remind us of them. We must accept our successes with humility and enjoy the good times with grace. My person with poise is Lee "Daddy" Brown. Daddy Brown is the Nashville Urban Director of the <u>Fellowship of Christian</u>

<u>Athletes</u>. Despite the circumstance, his tone of voice when responding to me is always comforting, yet stern. When he walks into a room, everyone seems to get the sense that everything will be fine. I've witnessed him have conversations with people who were frantic and on the brink of throwing in the towel of life. He remained poised and provided the reassurance that storms don't last forever. We all need those people who can calm us during calamity.

The old Welsh proverb says, "Without perseverance talent is a barren bed." The Dream Team member that embodies perseverance gives you that edge to remain persistent in the face of adversity. If you haven't already, find you a friend that has endured the toughest of times and moved forward as a champion. It's not enough to find a friend that has experienced tribulation. We all have tribulation. The person you want on your team is the one who has stood tall during turmoil and embraced the growth that results from the pain. Your person of perseverance can help you find ways to capitalize on the tough times. You don't want to simply go through the difficult moments; you want to grow as a result of them. These people are fighters and will help fight for your purpose. In the moments when quitting seems easier, the person of perseverance will remind you of the important role you play in the progression of the world around you.

Your platform is created through your purpose; however, it is anchored by the efforts of your Dream Team. Building a team of strong individuals gives you a solid foundation. Mentoring, as well as being mentored, is a catalyst for personal growth. Allow yourself to be supported by people who have your best interest and can move you from potential to purpose.

REFLECTION POINTS

Imagine this: Envision yourself falling backward from a ladder into the arms of your best friend. Why did you trust this particular person to catch you?

Answer this: Are you truly willing to be pushed out of your comfort zone from potential to purpose? Why?

Try this: Ask a friend to tell you what they believe to be your greatest weakness and your greatest strength. Identify the members of your Dream Team.

Mentor:
Mentee:
Person with passion:
Person with poise:
Person with perseverance:

4

Servant Leadership

"We have to humble ourselves and the way you do that is by serving other people," says Tim Tebow. In this quote, Tim describes one of the toughest challenges for the entire flock of mankind. Whether it is in sports, politics, dating, or any other area of life, learning to serve others can be a daunting task. Regardless of our age and stage of life, we train ourselves year after year to gain advantages over our peers, coworkers, and teammates by any means necessary. America's capitalistic economy promotes individualistic motives that often require people to forsake their peers in order to reach their goals. The truth is, servitude is the greatest price one can pay for success. The empathy of service leaves a lasting mark on people, and we are appreciative of those who chose to serve. Despite how strict or firm our lives cause us to be at times, we all enjoy the gushy feeling of being able to serve others. The ability to lead is prefaced by the ability to serve. The quality of a leader is defined by his or her ability to understand what it means to walk in the shoes of one of his or her followers. According to many Americans, Bill Clinton is arguably one of the most favorable presidents in United States history. Clinton was known for his philanthropic efforts that took note of the under- represented citizens of the country. The first bill signed by Clinton was the Family and Medical Leave Act of 1993. This eye-opening gesture during his first term would be the benchmark for his legacy as the leader for America. According to the Department of Labor, this bill allows most federal employees up to twelve weeks of unpaid leave during any twelve- month period in order to tend to the medical needs of immediate family or self. Upon return, the employee must receive the same position or an equivalent position with identical benefits, pay, and status. Clinton's effort to exhibit humility and affection for the masses exemplifies a leader that understands the importance of establishing a sense of empathy. To lead is to connect, and to connect is to bridge the void from your vantage point of vision to the beliefs of every individual you lead. John C. Maxwell says, "Don't lead from the organization's perspective, lead from the people's perspective." Despite the level, servant leadership is predicated on the leader being capable of getting his or her followers to believe in the vision. What better way to get them to believe than by serving?

In Barach and Eckhard's <u>Paradoxes of Leadership,</u> they define the *Paradox of Kinship*. This paradox is fashioned as an effort of leaders to be relatable to his or her followers. Establishing this kinship takes maximized effort because a leader must learn to be advanced enough to lead, yet close enough to relate. Growing up in a crime-saturated city, I oftentimes had to distance myself from the criminal acts of friends. Although I was well-aware of the dangers that surrounded their risky lifestyles, I was determined to remain the positive role model in many of their lives. I was subconsciously fighting a heavy-duty battle with the Paradox of Kinship. Many people failed at positively impacting the lives of my friends because they were looked at as outsiders. I knew the only way to salvage the hope of helping them was in our kinship. Many lives I hoped to impact, sadly fell through the cracks. However, other lives were impacted through the relationships that were built and maintained despite the rough seams that held us together. As a leader, strive to find the balance that enables you to separate far enough from the pack that others have a model to emulate; yet stay close enough to the pack that you can empathize with their journey. One of the most discouraging habits practiced by many leaders is the inconsideration to get their hands dirty with work that they often feel is "beneath" their calling. The sad part about this type of leader is that they are blind to this simple fact – without followers, leaders do not exist. Who would Oprah Winfrey have become without her producers, directors, or other members of her staff? The late John Wooden won ten national championships while coaching men's basketball at UCLA. How many would he have won without his players? Leadership is often viewed as a desperate need and necessity for the followers. Contrary to popular belief, leadership is earned through a leader's demonstration of servitude, humility, and character over time. Leadership is not telling people how to follow; rather it is showing people how to lead. A leader's consistency builds confidence amongst peers. Leaders must cultivate people's willingness to follow and this only happens by passing the test of time. This cultivation process involves giving unfailing effort to maintain a trueness to character. I will expound on consistency later in this chapter.

As a leader, it is vital that you never take pride in being a crutch for others. The old Chinese proverb quotes, "give a man a fish, feed him for a day. Teach a man to fish, feed him for a lifetime." This proverb could not be truer as it relates to leadership. Some leaders try to convince themselves that giving man a fish is the ultimate gesture of humility and servitude. This is true if one's heart is in the right place. However, some leaders want people to come back for fish every day as means to polish their own pride and create a sense of dependency that keeps people one step behind them. Leaders can often become idol-minded and corrupt the true sentiments of leadership. By shifting the focus from leadership to dependency, leaders can create a symbolic leash that allows the followers to go so far before they must return for nurturing or guidance. Countless battered women habitually return to abusive relationships because they have become so dependent on someone else for survival and they cannot recognize the illogical decisions they are continuously making. Some bosses withhold valuable, cultivating information from their employees in order to keep a glass ceiling over their heads. The evidence of sincere leadership can be captivated by the leader's effort to empower and encourage their followers to seek independence and the tools needed to maintain it. My childhood pastor, Bishop William S. Wright says "don't judge my leadership by how the church operates when I'm here, but judge my leadership by how the church operates when I'm not here." This stems from the ideology that true leadership can be measured in the manifestation of followers being capable of transitioning into effective leaders. Leaders can pinpoint weaknesses and make calculated efforts to eliminate them. True leaders possess the ability to be intentional about fine-tuning people's weakness in order to extract their potential. Too often people set out on journeys with no means to a desired end. Being goal oriented only takes you so far. Strategic methods to accomplish goals can often be created by good leaders that do not ignore the individual steps that lead to the top of the staircase. Servant leaders must be careful to properly analyze their relationships because the formula to success is not written in ink, but it must be erased and revised on a case-by-case basis.

Leaders must possess two extremely valuable traits in their role. Before anything, servant leaders must be willing to understand. This may sound offensively simple; however, this proves to be an extremely difficult practice for a countless number of leaders to follow. Understanding your followers does not happen overnight or in one conversation. At its root, the word *'understand'* means to have a thorough comprehension. Most leaders willingly put in rigorous efforts to gain a deeper understanding of everything surrounding their lives, except the most important thing. The people! This is baffling. Leaders of companies continually analyze their company's competition, budget, and goals. For some odd reason, most business leaders do not analyze the most essential part of their business…the people! Oftentimes, my college football coaches were guilty of the same prideful mishap. While breaking down film, creating scouting reports, and hauling in recruits, they exhibited the quintessential habits of college coaches. Because these habits consumed them, they did not plug into the lives of their players, as they should have. As a leader, it is important to invest into understanding the crowd that you lead. Just as with any other entity of life, understanding your followers is a time-consuming effort that requires an in-depth view of individuals as they relate to you and the common goal. Understanding people can be difficult because it takes an openness that most leaders are not willing to expose. Leaders are commonly perceived as mystical figures that cannot be broken. Many of them have mastered the poker face a result of this ideology. This is a total misconception. This leads to the next important trait leaders must possess, being relatable. Indeed, leadership has its times for the stone-faced expressions and abrupt demeanor because of the weight of responsibility carried by leaders. However, contrary to popular belief, leaders gain the most respect when they show natural humanness. Michael Jordan's legacy as a leader reached another dimension on Father's Day in 1996. This was the emotion packed moment when Jordan's Chicago Bulls family embraced him as he clinched his first championship after his father's murder in 1993. Now it was evident that even basketball's Superman was capable of shedding tears. Even now, the footage of Jordan rolling around on the floor of the United Center as he tightly hugs the trophy brings tears to people's eyes. For Jordan, his team, and his fans, this encirclement of support was simply the reciprocation of the devout leadership Jordan displayed every second he graced the basketball court. His service as a leader inspired his supporting cast to become his anchoring force during a tragedy that would cause looming instability for even the strongest of people. Franklin D. Roosevelt was in charge of leading a country that was hopeless at the time he took office. During his first 100 days in office, Roosevelt implemented the "New Deal". This effort involved the government's energies of revamping the economic status of the United States. Roosevelt reached down to aid those that had been stricken with poverty, unemployment, and foreclosures. Because of his willingness to serve the weakest links in the American chain, he is viewed as one of the greatest leaders in United States history. In fact, his leadership can be attested, as he is the only U.S. president to serve more than two terms. Martin Luther King Jr.'s leadership grew to soaring heights after he was forced to write letters from behind the bars of an Alabama jail cell. Dr. King overlooked the consequences of his actions and placed himself on the front line of the battlefield for civil rights. Although he was one of the most polarizing figures of his day, he focused his efforts on ensuring that society's highest and lowest citizens were given equal opportunity to human rights. It was King's strategic targeting of the wealth gap in America that prompted his assassination in 1968. After gaining ground on civil rights, he began to shift his focus to the wages of sanitation workers. King viewed their welfare no different from those of higher economic status. His commitment was undeniable and his followers became willing to tread his path that went against the grain of society.

As you move forward analyzing how you plan to carry the torch of leadership, be sure to ask yourself some key questions. Who defines leadership? This question is concerned with the assignment of leaders and the nature of their relationships. Leaders are created by two means: First, leaders can assume the role when there is an obvious void, and innate character inspires them to become the bridge for that breach. Or secondly, leadership can come by assignment. People often look for leaders to take the reins. If the reins dangle free from ownership for too long, people are not afraid to assign seemingly capable prospects.

When deciding to take the initiative of filling the void of leadership, be sure to step in with premier confidence. Confidence is reassuring to those around you. I've been able to witness many of my students become outstanding orators because of confidence. Initially, several of them have compared the anxiety of presenting a speech in front of peers to actual life and death circumstances. Although comical, the fear of public speaking is a theme of Americans. My common piece of advice is to be confident enough that the audience takes everything you say as truth. Whether the speech goes along as rehearsed or not, speak boldly with a demeanor of certainty. These same students use their fear of public speaking to master the art of confidence and actually become great speakers. Leaders must do the same. Never neglect substantial study and preparation, but mastering confidence can take you a long way. Believing that you possess what it takes to fulfill the duty of leadership is contagious. It doesn't take long for people to sense doubt and uncertainty. Stepping into a leadership role by your own intuition can backfire quickly if you don't believe in your own capabilities. Taking the dive into leadership should be an innate decision based on a prompt given from the heart. This gives ground for another point. This heartfelt decision is not to be confused with feelings. You will forever be troubled by choices made on feelings. Feelings are the rollercoaster of emotions that take place daily within all of us. Sometimes we're up and other times we're down. That's not a rollercoaster you want to ride as a leader. Giving in to emotions will open the door to the deepest forms of instability. Therefore, the confidence possessed by a leader who takes initiative is created by a true examination of the heart. The heart will not allow you to tiptoe away from your assignment. The urgent desire created by a true calling will not let you rest until your purpose is being fulfilled.

Being called into leadership is a totally different scenario. Maybe you do not feel any "pulls" at your heart's strings to step into that leadership role. That's perfectly fine. Everyone is not destined to be a leader. Additionally, you are not designed to be the leader in every facet of your life. Not all circumstances call for your leadership. Relish the opportunity to follow and learn from other leaders when the time calls for you be in the background. Trying to force yourself into leadership roles that are not in line with your purpose is a huge mistake. Don't be the overbearing person who cannot embrace a position that is not at the forefront. Nonetheless, there may be instances when your leadership characteristics shine through so brightly that someone else sees the need for you to step up to the plate. This very well may be an opportunity for leadership that you did not foresee. When in route to accomplishing goals, people depend on a leader to guide the direction of the unit. Even the finest of ships need a captain to stir. That's the nature of the human race; therefore, people are often promoted out of their comfort zone into the ranks of leadership. The key to this avenue of leadership is having a sense of ingenuity. Because you were assigned, it is evident that the unit needs a mind capable of establishing strategic tactics to reach the goals. It's not difficult for people to see the beauty of a finished painting. I think most people can identify a nice finished product. The problem is that most people don't know what type of brushes it takes to match the texture of the canvas. Others don't know how to properly mix colors to create the desired outcome. The nuances of the process are why people designate leaders. They can see the goal, but are blind to the strategic steps needed to reach that desired end. People who are inserted into leadership roles must master creativity. These leaders must value the foundation and get the people around them to be interested in the process. Assigned leaders must quickly show themselves to be assertive and capable because many people do not enjoy the pain of the process. Oftentimes when people don't see results instantly, they want to abort the mission. As a leader, it is your responsibility to redirect their vision from the top of the stairway to the first step.

    The underlying theme for both avenues to leadership is the importance of being prepared. Preparation eases the transition into leadership and those who fail to prepare are likely to crumble. Abraham Lincoln said, "Give me six hours to chop down a tree and I will spend the first four sharpening the ax." Preparation dictates whether your role as a leader will be described as fluid or friction. Leaders should certainly connect the dots with details specific to the situation and have action plans that create a ladder to the desired destiny. Preparation is time-consuming and rigorous. The details of preparation can be daunting, so many people run away from this stage of leadership. How bad do you want to fulfill your purpose? Is it bad enough for you to put hours upon hours of preparation into understanding and cultivating your gift? This book is about chasing your purpose because platform is a byproduct of purpose. Our platform is what we see as the glorious continuum of our existence. The fact of the matter is, preparation is what takes place when nobody knows your name. Preparation will test your discipline to differentiate between becoming the best leader versus becoming a better leader. There's only one best, but we all can become better. Your enthusiasm to prepare will determine the height of your leadership success. A critical sector of preparation relates to self-evaluation. As a leader, you must first give way to honest, self-critique. Taking an introspective look at the flaws you have can prevent you from the embarrassment of someone else pointing these flaws out for you. You must analyze the strengths and weakness of your leadership attributes before you can apply them.

The three cardinal R's of leadership are *Relational, Reliable* and *Resilient*. Whether your leadership approach is charismatic, robust, or a generous mixture of both; effective leadership can be funneled through these three filters. Superior to any attribute, leaders must be *relational*. Because leaders take on the responsibility of the whole unit, it is imperative that leaders find multiple paths to relate to both peers and subordinates. As previously discussed, true leadership is one's ability to escort others into maximizing their strengths as they minimize and eliminate their weaknesses. Leadership demands a sense of humility and a capability of making people comfortable. Each day, you wake up with the responsibility of promoting yourself well enough that people will be comfortable with their decision to follow you. It is similar to the life of a car salesman. Great car salesmen are masters of self-promotion. As prospective car buyers contemplate signing the dotted line, salesmen are shooting arrows at their heart. The moment prospective buyers fall in love with the salesman, falling in love with the car comes as second nature. Salesmen often treat prospective buyers to a cup of hot coffee or a bottle of cold water. This simple gesture penetrates the psyche of buyers. After all, it feels good to have someone offer you a beverage after a hard day at work. Salesmen follow-up with conversation aimed at learning more about the potential buyer and to generate positive vibes. At this point, buyers have placed the importance of the person as equal to or greater than the product. All of sudden, the doubts a consumer may have about the car seem to dwindle away. Why is that? As an apprehensive consumer, you have been convinced that the car salesman would not steer you in the wrong direction. Based on the relationship that was groomed from the time you stepped into the dealership, you have concluded that the salesman has your best interest at heart. As a leader, the first call of duty should be building relationships that result in people falling in love with you. People must first become attached to you as a person before they become attached to you as a leader. Allow transparency to precede pride and remain intentional about finding avenues to connect with people.

Building relationships that encourage people to follow your lead must be maintained by your proof of being reliable. *Reliability* is an attribute that describes the consistency of a leader's work. Failing to show consistency in every aspect of your leadership leaves voids for speculation. The moment doubt overcomes trust in the minds of people following your lead, is the moment your leadership has lost its legitimacy. There is no such existence of partial trust, and to pursue leadership without total trust is a vain journey. Followers want to know that the words of their leader will coincide with the actions of their leader. In addition, they want to know that the actions of their leader will coincide with the character of the unit. As a leader, you are the glowing representation of your unit. You may have the most brilliant ideas, but they are useless if they do not accurately represent those whom you lead. The entity you lead is relying on you to remain consistent with the values that represent the whole. A person can sit in the same chair for ten consecutive years without a problem. The person grows attached to the chair because the chair faithfully does its job of providing support. However, the person's every thought concerning that chair will change the moment it collapses. Although the chair proved its reliability for ten years, the person will lose all trust after the first incident of disaster. Now the person will either throw the chair away or give a thorough inspection before sitting down each time afterward. There have been countless leaders thrown away or doubted because of one infringement on their reliability. This is not a call to be perfect, rather it is a call to pursue perfection. Don't allow routine to tear you away from your roots. The tenants of reliability are usually built during the developmental stages of leadership. As we develop into leaders, we take great pride in making sure our actions are productive and progressive. This fresh mindset produces results and gives people confidence in your ability as a leader. Success can cause you to lose this zeal. When success turns into complacency, it's easy to lose the fundamental traits of leadership that brought success to begin with. Always strive to stand on the core values that lie central to your purpose and who you are.

There is a special attraction to people who possess an undeniable fortitude to triumph. For most people, winning is an option.

The great leaders believe winning is the only option. Leaders must be *resilient*! Effective leadership requires an untamable grit that continuously pushes people to their full capacity. The backbone of a leader lies in his or her ability to overcome shortcomings that often discourage others from remaining progressive in their pursuit of goals. Don't be a circumstantial leader. Our society already has enough people who embrace leadership when it's convenient, and deflect leadership when it's tough. We need more leaders who are unafraid to boldly face adversity and stay the course. Even dead fish can go with the flow, but not everybody is willing to swim against the current. The great innovator, Elon Musk says, "When something is important enough, you do it even if the odds are not in your favor." Sometimes there won't be any evidence in your favor. There may not be any hints of success for what you desire to do as a leader. Better yet, what if there is no blueprint or success story that precedes your vision? You may be an innovator or inventor of new ideas. Don't let the odds deter you from moving forward with the vision God has granted you. Do you possess the resilience it takes to scratch and claw your way to success? As you take on leadership, be sure to deeply anchor an abundance of tenacity within your heart. Every route to success has multiple detours and obstacles that will force you to make a decision to persist or quit. Resilient leadership flows downhill and produces organizations, companies, and teams that refuse to be denied of their goals.

REFLECTION POINTS

Imagine this: Imagine creating every relationship with a foundation of trust and communication.

Answer this: Who is the greatest leader you know? What attributes of leadership do they possess that have given them success?

Try this: Write down <u>1</u> task you desire to complete each month. Create a short list of action items that will help you accomplish that goal. As you complete each action item, check it off the list.

5

Weight Lifting

Some of my fondest memories of playing college football are specific moments inside the weight room. The most intense days in the weight room were "max-out" days. These days were designed to test the incremental changes in each athlete's maximum capacity for a variety of bodily functions. These days were highly anticipated and always ended in jubilation or defeat. When increasing your max, it became reassuring that your hard work was paying off. When decreasing or maintaining the same max, it was typically a sign that somewhere along the way, you were lacking in commitment. Watching my teammates max-out became one of the most contrasting displays of emotion that life could offer. Their facial expressions would illicit signs of despair and anguish for a few excruciating seconds. All of sudden, a successful weight increase would produce smiles that Colgate and other toothpaste manufacturers would be proud to endorse. These smiles were often coupled with screams of excitement.

Not once did any of my teammates regret the brief moments of anguish that gave them prolonged moments of satisfaction. In route to your success, there will be some heavy opposition that requires some moments of agony and pain. There are only a handful of promises that people can make with 100 percent assurance that it will come true. Oppositions and obstacles will surely arise in all of our lives. That's one promise that will live forever. The most accomplished, affluent, and influential people to ever walk the face of this earth faced heavy opposition and resistance to their goals. When speaking with my former high school teammate and NFL All-Pro, Dontari Poe, he said, *"I just had to overcome with all the negative stuff happening around me. It wasn't about the negatives in my life that were going on, it was about me working as hard as I can through all the adversity to make it out of the negativity and create a positive situation for my family and I. I had tunnel vision."* Success dare not come without a price. When you find yourself excluded from tribulation, pinch yourself because it is definitely a dream or you are doing something wrong. One lesson I learned from the experiences in the weight room was that the individuals who relentlessly fought the weight, despite the struggle, would prevail. The individuals who allowed the strains of struggle to overcome their desire to lift the weight would experience defeat until someone assisted them. This reflects the two opposing mindsets people possess when facing life's "weights." There is a very condensed group of people who are willing to strain their way to goals, regardless of how resistant life may prove to be. Their life will be marked by moments that reflect the fruits of their labor. They will reap the benefits of never quitting. On the contrary, life provides a much more attractive route for those who are not willing to face the archery of antagonism. Bowing down to life's oppositions forces you to relinquish your purpose. Giving up during life's heavy moments is an indication that your pain outweighs your purpose. At that point, you have decided that you would rather allow life to control you like a puppet. One of the most discouraging moments in the weight room is looking into the eyes of your teammate for help with the weight you could not conquer. Because you could not generate enough energy to lift the weight, you become dependent on someone else to lift the weight for you. Why settle for life giving you a helping hand? It's time for you to become the helping hand to others. You have so much to offer the world; don't let the weights win!

One of the most challenging weights of life is tragedy. The tears of tragedy can drown dreams. Tragedy often causes people to lose sight of their goals. If not properly managed, the perplexity that surrounds tragedy will deceive you into the misconception that nobody else has experienced such pain. However, truth is, no one eludes tragedy. I would be remiss to avoid taking a moment to cover such a heavy topic for fear of making you recycle scars, tears, and pain that you may have suppressed. There are three reasons the burdens of tragedy are difficult to manage. The first of those reasons is that tragedy often makes a grand entrance into our lives during moments where we seemingly have all of our 'ducks in a row.' We all spend our lives attempting to organize and plan events for our benefit. We make plans spiritually, physically, and financially to set ourselves on track to enjoy the gift of life. You have your own personal standard of what it means to be moving in the right direction. We all desire to live a life of order and stability. The sting of tragedy would lose a significant amount of venom if we were able to prepare and brace ourselves for the blow. However, life tends to prefer surprise rather than script. Just when you feel that you've mapped out the next phase of your life, here comes an unforeseen event that quickly alters your world. Right after you have paid off your credit card or repaired your car, here comes a devastating blow that makes those things seem minimal or vain. The untimely arrival of tragedy is not something you can get accustomed to. It's during these moments when you have a heavy heart that you must pick yourself up to keep moving forward. Also, tragedy often displaces us from our comfort zone. There are countless ways this happens, but is usually felt most with the addition or change of responsibilities. As previously mentioned in Chapter 2, most of us live life by routine. We know our responsibilities and we create patterns to ensure we are able to stay on course to fulfill those obligations. During tragic moments, we are often obligated to fulfill responsibilities that place us in unfamiliar territory. Unknown territory is a place where you have not been or had no plans to go. I think we all can attest that unknown territory is a scary place to gain responsibility. Maybe your family places you in charge of planning the funeral of a loved one. In addition to mourning your loss, you are also faced with an added responsibility. Or maybe you have to renovate your home after it is ripped apart by inclement weather. Now you have added responsibility of following protocol with your insurance company or hiring contractors. You also gain financial duties to fulfill the responsibility of this unfamiliar territory. The point is, new responsibility looks different for everyone in the midst of tragedy. Thirdly, tragedy is such a heavy weight because it lingers. Tragedy can take many forms, but the common thread is the lasting effect that remains afterward. Each day presents another reminder of the misfortune. Closing the chapter to tragedy has no outline and will forever be a large pill to swallow. No matter the coping strategies you decide to apply, never let this next statement escape you. Do not get stuck in tragedy! One fundamental mistake so many of us make is allowing misfortune to consume our destiny. Live with it, don't die by it. The grip of tragedy will squeeze you lifeless if you allow the wounds to remain open. Too often people view scars in a negative way. Here's what's important about scars – they only come when you are healed! Again, tragedy impacts us all during our lifetime, but learning to live with scars will free you from becoming stagnant. Allowing chapters to close in your life is so important to your continual growth. Tragedy hurts badly enough, so why allow those wounds to remain open? Scars are a sign that you have overcome the pain. Those scars may remain forever, but they will only be a reminder that you are no longer bound by the hurt of tragedy.

It is very crucial that you limit the power of tragedy by recognizing reality. The misfortune and pain of tragedy create walls of bitterness and fatigue. However, it is your choice to climb these walls to escape from being caved in by calamity. If you allow the effects of tragedy to hang over your head, these walls can escalate to insurmountable heights that prevent you from seeing your way out. Recognizing reality is overcoming the uncanny instinct we have as humans to pity ourselves in a way that gives us a justification for selfishness. Tragedy often becomes an avenue for people to justify lying down to the pressures of life. This leads to giving up. Sadly, some people delight in misfortune in order to gain the sympathy of others. Don't let that be you! We all need the stability of a supporting cast during droughts in our lives; nevertheless, do not forget how to pour your own glass of water with the rain. Once you recognize that tragedy is harsh, yet common across humanity, it is imperative to refocus your vision. I learned from experience that it is tremendously dangerous to drive while continuously looking in the rear-view mirror. When your goals are ahead of you, and your focus is on the past, disaster is eminent. As tough as it may be to leave tragedy behind, it is necessary for progress. Am I suggesting to forcefully suppress the pain and agony of tragedy? By no means would I suggest or imply such apathy. In fact, life's rear-view mirror gives you the luxury of peeking back to remember the road you have overcome. Meanwhile, at the finish line, your goals continue to wait along with your destiny. In his song "How High", rapper J. Cole says, "Life is a movie, pick your own role, climb your own ladder or dig your own hole; Sitting around crying is like sitting around dying, if you want to touch the sky I bet you'll figure out flying." Cole highlights a fundamental principle for success–taking responsibility. We live in a society that teaches us how to create excuses. While pursuing purpose, we should make conscious efforts to minimize excuses. Using excuses becomes a habit and we find ourselves justifying reasons to quit. These lines of Cole's song run parallel to conquering tragedy. Either you can allow tragedy to become another rung on your ladder to destiny or you can experience the detriment of sulking in pain. Whichever turn you take at that fork in the road is up to you, but both roads have a future that is a direct correlation of the decision you make at the fork.

Another weight of life that often overcomes unprepared people is the pressure created by family and friends. Companionship is beautiful, but the maintenance is taxing. As a senior in high school, I fell in love with famed pop singer, Beyoncé. I had no problem blasting her music through my speakers and singing along with her word for word. She's had a remarkable career and I'm glad to say that I have been able to see her in concert. The experience was like no other concert I've ever witnessed. Her stage presence and charisma are breathtaking. She couples the intense choreography with incredible vocal consistency. As I watched her perform, I took note of the people around me. Spectators were torn between whether to dance to her every beat or sing to her every word. It was amazing to see so many people in awe of the way she graced the stage. As Beyoncé peered out into the audience, I could only imagine the thoughts that she had about the crowd being a witness to the finished product. In order to deliver such astonishing performances, she puts in hours of time and energy that we never see. In several interviews, she reveals that her success is a product of her tireless work ethic to perfect her craft. The same effort characterizes effective relationships. The energy to keep relationships coherent can overcome you at times. All of us have our unique nuances that make us complex individuals. Therefore, relationships are an unending effort to properly handle the complexities of people well enough to accomplish goals. This means there will be people who easily mesh with your temperament, preferences, and habits. On the other hand, there will be others who don't. The road of least resistance is to avoid all people who don't easily sync with you. You must push back against that ideology. With that mindset, it will be hard to get things done. Beyoncé could avoid every dance movement or high note that causes her to work a little harder. Instead, she invests hours of hard work until those challenges become second nature. Some people in our lives will be major challenges. Many of these people we can avoid with the strategies we learned about our *Dream Team*, but others we must lace up our boot straps to manage effective relationships.

Family and friends may be by your side, but they're not necessarily on your side. As the old saying goes, "misery loves company." It's unfortunate, but most of your family and friends will not capitalize on life and reach their goals. Most people never reach the platform of their destiny.

However, it's more unfortunate that they can often become your primary resistance in route to your providential future. Whether overt or unintentional, the people closest to you can present the heaviest opposition in your life. People may tell you that you're acting differently from your past. Embrace that! You were never meant to remain the same. Only dead things stop growing. They may claim you think you're too good for them. Smile! Smiling fights more battles than you think. A smile goes a long way and often forces negative energy to leave! They may even tell you that you're not going to succeed. Prove them wrong! The fire for success that burns in your heart should be fueled by the sparks of skepticism. As mentioned previously, the relationships that anchor your life should bear good fruit. If not, lift that weight from your life by cutting down the trees that are not producing good fruit.

The boundaries of all relationships either hinder or promote progress. The establishment of proper boundaries is essential for ridding yourself of unnecessary burdens. It's too often that we entangle ourselves with weights not meant for us to carry. Life will give you enough challenges, so don't create more burdens for yourself. If given the opportunity to take advantage of one-sided relationships, people will. Unilateral (one-sided) giving has its place. There should be times in all of our lives in which we should give freely without any regard for reciprocity. Benevolent giving is one of the most rewarding gestures one can experience. However, allowing people to violate your boundaries to the point of taking advantage of you is one of the most draining experiences you can endure. Though it may serve as a disappointment, the harsh reality is that there are relationships that are not worth forming. One Valentine's Day, my girlfriend at the time bought me a very nice pair of shoes. I owned a jacket that had been hanging untouched in my closet for months because I didn't have anything to wear with it, but these new shoes changed that. While packing my suitcase for an educational convention in Florida that spring, I brainstormed on what clothes I would wear on the plane. Excited to flaunt my new shoe and jacket combination, of course, the decision was fairly simple. The weather in Middle Tennessee, where I was living, was cool and windy at the time. This made my wardrobe choice a perfect fit. However, upon arriving in Florida, I quickly became aware of the climate change. Walking outside in Orlando, Florida was not as comfortable as back home in Tennessee, where temperatures were much cooler. Despite the discomfort of slowly getting hotter by the minute, the excitement of wearing my jacket with my new shoes made me keep it on. Then I came to the mental intersection that is familiar to us all… is it worth it? The answer to this question was not complex and I decided I had enough. I nearly ripped my jacket off. My pseudo-fashionable moment was not worth the discomfort. My crossroads moment liberated me from an uncomfortable, unproductive situation that I did not have to take on. Will you make the right decision at your crossroads for upholding or restructuring your boundaries? In most cases, we control the relationships and burdens that we take on. Maybe relationships are the perfect fit for you at one point in your life, similar to my jacket being perfect for the weather in Tennessee. However, you do not have climate control of your life, so you have to make adjustments to what is feasible during different seasons in your life. Dealing with the irritation of unnecessary sweat underneath my jacket drove me to make a decision that was best for me. We know when relationships with our family, friends, and our significant others become unhealthy for our wellbeing. The key is learning how to cut off the circulation to those unproductive ties. Boundaries keep the healthy, necessary elements in. Simultaneously boundaries filter unhealthy, unnecessary elements out. You have to truly picture your boundaries as a fence and take time to evaluate what should be on your side of the fence and what should remain on the exterior. Overcomplicating who should be on your side of the fence can be avoided by asking yourself this simple question: Is this person helping me to fulfill my purpose? Any reservation or doubt that keeps this answer from being a "yes," is likely an indication that this person should not be among the privileged people on the interior of your fence. Odds are, we all have trespassers on our property! Remember, your purpose is your platform. What does this mean as it relates to boundaries? If people aren't connected to your purpose, then they should not be connected to your platform. There will be people that want to have a place in your life when they feel you are successful. Those people are chasing an opportunity to be connected to the superficial feeling of being "on top." When you are elevated by your purpose and given a platform to the world, there will be people coming from all walks of life seeking a relationship. Many will be from your past. People you haven't heard from in years tend to become very concerned when your dreams start becoming reality. Those people that didn't answer your calls or emails will start to reach out to you. Be careful! Purpose is specific and intentional. Those who are not connected to that purpose should remain outside of your fence.

Life has people, places, and things that create heaviness. Pressures will tempt you to quit before you ever reach your potential. As you've read, there are some problems, such as tragedy, that can't be avoided. We all experience tragedy. However, there are other burdens, like people that we can sidestep. Even if we can't sidestep those relationships, we can learn to manage people in order to continue moving forward with efficiency.

The weights of life that are beyond your control must be fought. Furthermore, the weights of life that are within your control should be avoided. Lift the weights, get stronger, and keep going.

REFLECTION POINTS

Imagine this: Think about what the world loses if you decide to quit on your purpose.

Answer this: Who are the toxic people that need to be extracted from your life?

Try this: Encourage people facing tragedy to live with it and not die by it. Draw a circle. On the inside of the circle, write the names of the people who are connected to your purpose. On the outside of the circle, write the names of the people who are <u>not</u> connected to your purpose and need to be on the exterior of your boundary fence.

Your Purpose Is Your Platform

6

Momentum Swing

Murphy's Law states, "Anything that can go wrong, will go wrong." That can definitely be an intimidating thought. The rigid reality of this theory is best combatted with preparation and anticipation of the *momentum swings* that will undoubtedly take place in your life. As a former athlete and avid sports fan, it is exhilarating to witness how momentum can swing during sporting events. In most sporting events, one team initially establishes their edge and the momentum of competition is in their favor. This team may vigorously battle to maintain their edge or may just have clear-cut dominance. Either way, one team usually finds a way to start well and make strategies go as planned. It is such a comfortable place to be when everything you have worked hard to establish, falls into alignment and gives you a sense of deserved reward. After all, hard work does pay off! All is well until things shift in the other direction. One incomparable moment is the feeling of your heart dropping from elation to panic as the tables turn and you are no longer able to enjoy the comfort of watching the plan unfold in perfect harmony. For me as a quarterback, one of the most demoralizing momentum changers was throwing an interception. There is nothing like leading your team down the field for what looks to be a sure score, only to have the drive abruptly ended by an interception. Now the other team begins to use this mistake as a catapult for their momentum. These momentum swings are not reserved for sports only; because life deals its fair share of momentum swings as well. Momentum swings are unique due to how quickly circumstances change from one extreme to another. These moments are characterized by an alarming shift from glee to doom that takes your breath away because of how fast it unfolds. After momentum swings in your life, you can respond one of two ways. Either you will accept that momentum has shifted and wait until the pendulum swings in your favor again. Or, you will return to the fundamentals that initially resulted in success and fight to get your ship back on course.

As circumstances push your life off course and knock your ducks out of row, it is important to revert back to your purpose. Your purpose places momentum on your side to begin with, but it is vital to quickly reconcile yourself to that purpose during times of momentum change. We all are guilty of losing sight of our purpose at different junctures of life. During the tough times when the tide turns against you, it is imperative that you return to the fundamentals. My high school had the only Aviation program in the city of Memphis, but I never took time to invest in that academic path because I had no intentions of becoming a pilot. Too often, we tend to educate ourselves solely on information that we assume can be beneficial to our personal lives. That's why it is important to take hold of the elements described in *Chapter 2, Stretching*. Don't let your life take place in a box. It was later in my life, as I boarded an airplane, that I learned the creed for aircraft pilots: *Aviate, Navigate, Communicate.* In the short conversation with this particular pilot, I gained some valuable insight. This emergency protocol we discussed became so personal to me because it highlights the character traits of an overcomer. *Aviate* is a reference to maintaining control of the aircraft. Despite the circumstance or type of emergency, every pilot's number one priority is to fly the airplane. Regardless of the stormy clouds ahead, fly the plane. Even with a bad signal from Air Traffic Control, fly the plane. Pilots go to school and endure hours of training to fly aircrafts; therefore, they are among the elite family of people that possess the skill-set to properly guide an aircraft from takeoff to landing. When disaster strikes, the first rule, *Aviate*, reminds pilots to remember the basics and remain focused on the initial task. The next time momentum swings in your life, take a moment to find the eye of the storm and relax. As hard as it may be to fathom, there is always a central point of peace in the midst of the worst storms. Anchoring down in this sanctuary of hope will allow you to endure until storms pass. People allow their journey to be derailed by focusing on life's uncomfortable shifts and forgetting the basic tactics that reproduce success. These are the people that accept the *momentum swing* and wait for the breeze of success to blow their way again. This doesn't have to be you. *Momentum swings* often occur because our culture has dropped the ball on equipping people with the fundamentals of reproducing success. Our educational system is widening that void by depending on a test-based curriculum designed for students to prove their academic progress by sufficient scoring on standardized tests. In essence, we are centering the need for preparation on a final summative assessment opposed to promoting the skills needed to reproduce mastery in various aspects of life. For this reason, it is crucial to hone in on the ability to reproduce success by developing character traits that cover the scope of challenges our youth will face. Then it doesn't become about reaching a goal and pressing restart, but it becomes a continuous routine of striving for daily triumph. With progressive character traits, you become responsive to *momentum swings* and reject the passive nature of awaiting success to cycle back to you. This responsive nature elicits control of your circumstance and you continue to *Aviate*. You are the pilot of your life, maintain control and fly!

The second facet of the pilot disaster protocol reminds pilots to *Navigate*. A pilot's ability to fly is insignificant without the knowledge of a destination. Exercising to remain healthy is one staple in my life. My goal is to exercise a minimum of four times a week. Although I thoroughly enjoy training, I've never been a fan of running for long distances. I much rather run a few short sprints and call it a day. As a challenge to myself, I began running miles. At first, I'd go to the gym, hop on the treadmill, and run a mile. One day, opposed to visiting the gym, I decided to run around my apartment complex until I made it back home. This was so much more exhilarating and didn't seem to be such a grueling task! Running on a treadmill can simulate running miles upon miles, but cannot reproduce the feeling of running with a destination in mind. When I set my mind that I will not stop running until I reach a predetermined finish line, I am able to stay zoned into my initial purpose because I have an end goal. I cannot see the finish line for most of the run, but I know it's there. As a passenger on a plane, the view from a window is rather unexpressive 20 minutes or so after takeoff. You can either peer into the bright blue skies of the day or the deep dark skies of the night. Either way, the immense skies around you are void of the intricate detail that you can see just after takeoff. No buildings, no trees, no cars. Although you cannot see your location at this point, there is an expectation that you will eventually arrive at your chosen destination. We all reach a point in our life that has a blurred view of the future. We set out to reach certain goals, but we often get lost in the vast reality of responsibilities after we take off to pursue them. This is when you should learn to *Navigate*. It's fairly simple to pursue goals when you can see the runway beneath you and everything seems to be lined up for you to land at your destination. The true test of character and grit comes when you're not exactly sure where the runway is and you get lost in everything around you. This is when it seems that your destination is purposely eluding you. Pilots depend on a radar system and air traffic control for guidance while navigating towards the destination. You should too! Your radar should be a detailed map of your destination and more importantly the route taken to arrive. Creating perfect sketches is the most prominent mistake people make when planning their life. There is minimal likelihood that "Plan A" will work to perfection. We all would love for our life to unfold in a manner that goes exactly as we plan, but I'm willing to argue that the odds of winning the lottery are higher. Peyton Manning was not considered a football genius because he executed perfect plays. He is a football genius because he accounted for the possibility that things could go wrong on any given play and found an alternate route to give his team success. In other words, although coaches game-plan strategies to counter Manning's attack, Manning has already prepared a counter-attack for the worst predicaments. If you never outline the steps taken to reach your goals, you're just running on a treadmill. You may be taking steps, but you're not going anywhere. It is important that you create a map that gives you detailed directions to make certain that your radar gives alerts anytime you are off route. The knowledge of steps taken towards goals separates the cream from the crop. Everyone has goals, but only those who create strategic routes to travel towards them will experience the manifestation of reaching those goals. Most would suggest creating some form of a three-year, five-year, and ten-year plan. That often puts the horse too far in front of the carriage. Goals are reached by winning daily. As a high school teacher, I stressed to my students the importance of seizing the day. With their bright eyes glued on the future, they oftentimes neglected the beauty of present opportunities. We are all guilty of this. Setting daily goals creates a sense of self-accountability. By no means would I promote discarding the goals for years ahead, but the downside to setting goals years in advance is the nonchalant attitude taken towards the smaller steps that allow you to reach those goals. There is no immediate opportunity for failure when your nearest goal is years away. However, by setting daily goals, you create a sense of urgent ownership for yourself. Mapping out those daily goals gives you prime responsibility for being proactive oppose to passive. Failing to accomplish daily goals should give you a boost of intrapersonal desire to win on a daily basis against your biggest opponent... yourself. Without a radar, we will turn our non-stop flight to our destination into one characterized by layovers and heavy turbulence. Know where you're going and create a navigation plan that ensures your arrival.

Communication is the last notch of disaster protocol for pilots. The ability to effectively *communicate* is pivotal during life's momentum swings. Communication can take place without being effective. All communication is not good communication. Communication is simply an exchange of ideas and information that involves a connection between two or more people. Making this exchange effective involves being intentional about the strategies utilized to convey the message. There is a great cloud of naivety and immaturity surrounding people that forsake the counsel of others. Pilots would be in big trouble without a means of communication with someone with the ability to help them. By all means, we should take on our goals head to head, but this shouldn't be exhibited in the form of loneliness. To remain on course, it is important that someone aside from yourself knows your desired destination. It is often our lines of communication that reel us back on track. If we could predict the outcome of each day, our lives would be calculated to the point that we could survive on our own. The inconsistencies of life, that put us on our back at times, are justification for a helping hand. *Communicate* during times of despair! Those despairing times create many victims that fall prey to the idea that we have to wait for momentum to swing back in our favor. Champions create the momentum swing and reject the passivity of defeat! Shifting the atmosphere of your life cannot take place without effective communication with those in positions to help you. Air traffic control workers are in place to aid pilots during tough segments of the flight when pilots are unable to maintain stability of the aircraft. The presence of the air-traffic controller is in vain if the pilot is unwilling to communicate the need. The unique part about the relationship between the pilot and the Air Traffic Control Center is the fact that the pilot never has to relinquish ownership of the aircraft. It is perfectly fine to be intimate with your goals and delight in owning the pursuit of attaining them. Although the ownership of the pursuit is yours to own, it is important not to become irresponsibly overprotective of your dreams. It can be toxic! Even if the Air Traffic Control Center has to aid in directing the aircraft, the pilot is still the chief of the flight. You will always be the chief of your dreams. Do not be so selfish that you chose to be helpless. Communication is a healthy choice and a sign of maturity. Failure to communicate is a side effect of senseless pride.

Momentum Swings give a glaring reminder of why the pursuit of dreams should be predicated on inspiration and purpose. Pushing against the grain of a *momentum swing* takes maximized, consolidated effort. Even in its simplest state, running takes effort. Running against the wind takes an effort that makes us realize the importance of uniformity that takes place in our bodily functions. Running into the wind causes us to utilize much more exertion to ensure that our movements are harmonious in propelling us forward. It takes this same concentrated desire to redirect momentum swings. You will not be up for the challenge if vain rewards are the motivation for you to turn things around. The burning desire to recapture control of your dreams has to be connected to substantial inspiration or the pursuit is likely to fizzle away. Ask yourself this question about how your heart burns to turn momentum back in your favor. Does my heart burn like a campfire that can be doused with a bucket of water? Or does my heart burn like a forest fire that will burn for years despite every effort of people, obstacles, and circumstances that attempt to inhibit my growth?

REFLECTION POINTS

Imagine this: Envision the world if everyone gave up on his or her dreams when something went wrong.

Answer this: What habits can you change in order to win your daily battles in route to success? What habits can you begin in order to win your daily battles in route to success?

Try this: Designate a time at the end of each day to note how you moved closer to a specific goal.

7

The Moment You Have Waited For

There's a point in time when opportunity meets preparation. There's a day that will come in which the very opportunity you wished for will present itself. There will be a moment to arise that gives you a window of time to step into greatness by converting your preparation into production. What will happen in that quiet moment when you have the opportunity to run with your dream? Will you be overwhelmed by fear and uncertainty? Will the whispers of doubt discourage you from standing boldly to move forward? Truth is, we create every excuse of why things won't work instead of envisioning the reasons they will.

Each day I remind myself that yesterday is a testimony; tomorrow is a hope, and today is a chance. We must value today. Living in the moment of opportunity grants us what neither yesterday or tomorrow can offer– a present chance. You have a present chance to start a business. You have a present chance to apply for your dream job. You have a present chance to pursue your degree. You have a present chance to find a spouse. The possibilities are endless. However, opportunity comes with a decisive responsibility. The decision to move forward with opportunity is your choice. At this point, there must be a filter of all doubt and uncertainty and a strong desire to see your platform come to fruition. Success and doubt cannot be birthed from the same person. A person with uncertainty about their ability to accomplish their goals must sift through this doubt until success is the only option. When it comes to reaching your goals, you do not want options. I've always been told to shoot for the stars. The latter part of that statement says, "If you fail, you will land on a cloud." I've come to realize that I do not view this proverbial claim like most people. This statement makes me uncomfortable because it ordains failure as an option. When reaching for the stars, you should not give yourself the option to fall on a cloud. After all, the cloud is not the destination you desire, so why should you become satisfied with landing there? You shouldn't! If your desire is to reach a star, remove the satisfaction of landing on a cloud from your mind. If a star is your desire, whether you land on a cloud or on the ground, you have fallen short of your goal. In my eyes, there is only one way for this cliché statement to come alive. The moment you land on that cloud, it is time to return to the drawing board and construct a plan to get from that cloud to the star you desired from the beginning. Whether you have to swing like Tarzan from cloud to cloud until you reach the star or if you must build your own personal spaceship, do not neglect the destination for the satisfaction of a moral victory. People around you will often promote that effort equals success. In my first year as a high school broadcasting teacher, there was one student who worked harder than any other student in my class. He came to class and took excellent notes that were usually accompanied by excellent questions. He never failed to complete assignments on time. His attitude in class was always exemplary and he often tried to prepare the atmosphere for learning. The only problem this student faced was his inability to convert this preparation on test day. Although his efforts were tremendous, he often failed to seize the opportunity for success. As I mentioned before, I'm not a fan of tests being the only evaluation of a student's success. However, regardless of my thoughts on the need for educational reform, I wanted my students to excel with the current education standards. After expressing to him the need for improving his test grades, I gave him strategies to "seize the moment." As a teacher, I could not give him an "A" on the test simply because he worked hard. My expectations for him to prove his mastery on test day were equal to every other student in my class. I dare not pat him on the back for only striving for "A's" on tests. We all are supposed to give our best efforts anyway. However, I patted him on the back as encouragement to persevere until making "A's" became a habit. Because I did not let him become content with landing on a cloud, he began to aim higher and higher until "A's" were the only choice for him. He learned to turn the strain of his preparation into the success of his product.

The beauty of opportunity is not in the fact that you are given a chance to succeed. However, the beauty lies in the fact that you have a perfect chance to prove that your journey of preparation was not in vain. In an age when social media is one of the staples of everyday life, people so often voice how hard they are working to the public. For some reason, people feel that publicly vocalizing their everyday quest to succeed brings them closer to their goals. I will not resent these overt acts, but truth is, there will be a perfect time to prove how hard you have actually worked. There will undoubtedly come a moment in time when you cannot point the finger of blame at anyone. That moment will arise that you dreamt about. In this pressing time, you will respond by *"attacking"* or *"reacting."* Players attack, spectators react. "Attacking" opportunity involves taking steps towards your goal that take you from being a spectator to being a player. At sporting events, players create the memorable moments, make the big plays, and establish the atmosphere of the venue. Fans simply react to what the players are doing. When opportunity comes calling, it is your moment to attack and create the memorable moments for yourself. For those who are not prepared for this moment, attacking will seem like a risk. However, for those who have prepared, attacking becomes a thrill. When you land that interview with the company of your dreams, don't sit as a spectator while they put you on the hot seat. Attack the interview and make the employer answer tough questions as well. Don't simply send your resume to generic websites; make a follow-up call to express your desire to fill a position. Maybe, you can't find anyone that believes enough in your idea to give you money; fundraise! You may experience being cut from a team or let go from a job. This is the moment you should fight to erase your weaknesses and sharpen your strengths. Simply said, do not accept the notion that you have to be carried wherever the wind of life blows you. Anchor down to your desires and do not let any circumstance uproot you from your destiny.

Fear is the most crippling emotion to anyone's dreams. There are so many variations of fear connected to chasing dreams, but they can be bottled into three categories: *Fear of Failure*, *Fear of Rejection*, and *Fear of Change*. When you take a moment to analyze the presence of fear, you begin to realize that its presence is very predictable. Fear never presents itself when you are in the comfort of routine and monotony. Fear doesn't tend to bother you in the midst of daily tasks. The paralysis of fear manifests during moments of opportunity. Those opportune moments in your life when you are on the brink of accomplishment and attainment will likely always be interrupted by public service announcements made by fear. The question is, will you listen to those whispers of fear?

Fear of Failure can cause the most gifted people in the world to be strangled by mediocrity. This type of fear is characterized by the thoughts of defeat outweighing the thoughts of victory. The result of someone pulling a trigger on a gun is the firing pin being ignited. The firing pin then ignites the primer. In turn, the primer ignites the powder. Milliseconds after this process takes place, a bullet exits the gun. The detail of this process is a mouthful for someone that does not do target practice as a hobby or have a keen familiarity with firearms. However, everyone can recognize the process results in a product that cannot take place without first pulling the trigger. In this process, you don't manually ignite the firing pin, the primer, or the powder. These are all results of the trigger being pulled. Processes that define our life unfold in a similar manner. The exciting knowledge of life is that there are so many goals you are destined to accomplish, but will you allow the fear of not accomplishing them prevent you from taking the initial step? As a football fanatic, I have watched Tom Brady lead his team on game-winning drives year after year. The fearless Brady distinctly orchestrates a group of ten other men with the demeanor of a lion in the jungle. Lions may not be exactly sure what they will eat for their meal. In fact, these big cats oftentimes are unsure of exactly how they will hunt down their prey during the next kill. Nevertheless, one fact remains in the thought process of lions. They are positive that when they are hungry, they will eat! One late night I perused through the channels of my television and nothing grabbed my attention. I decided to watch National Geographic On Demand and I was in for a treat. One particular episode still resonates freshly in my memory. Intriguing as my favorite animal, lions always seem to shackle my attention. As I learned about the Xakanaxa lion pride, that roamed the safari of Africa, nothing amazed me more than their fearless nature. In 2008, the African safari experienced a period of drought that drove many animals into starvation. As the usual prey for the Xakanaxa pride ventured to new territory for nourishment, the opportunities for food became scarce for the lions. Lions don't prefer to hunt massive land animals like buffalo and elephants because of the difficulty and danger of the kill; however, they prefer to hunt animals that don't pose such a difficult fight upon catching. I developed a sense of sorrow for the lions as I watched them vainly search for food during this period of drought. When the drought seemed to take a turn for the worst, the lions turned the tide. The Xakanaxa lion pride made a decision to either die from starvation or rally together to kill an elephant that would be a very dangerous opponent to take down. Knowing that elephants were extremely massive prey and there was a chance that the hunt could end fatally, the rulers of the safari made up in their mind that fear was not going to separate them from the opportunity to change their life. With a careful, confident approach and a few successful leaps, the lions corralled a massive elephant and had themselves dinner on the safari.

Although the elephant was not as easy of a kill as they were accustomed to, the lions made a conscious decision to trample fear and take control of their well-being. Their choice to step outside of their comfort zone only came when the thought of failure was overshadowed by their desire to change their current situation. During game-winning drives, Tom Brady doesn't know exactly how his team will score. However, his aura says that he is sure that his team will find a way, just as the lions decide they will eat by any means necessary. In our lives, there has to come a moment when we remind ourselves that there is a process of success that cannot begin unless we have the boldness to pull the trigger. Brady couldn't lead his team with the fear of making a mistake that will cost his team the game. There are countless scenarios that could put Brady on the losing end of attempting to lead his team to success. In fact, Brady has made mistakes during his career that have arguably costs his team the game on several occasions. Even with times of failure in his history, Brady only envisions the game-winning drive ending in success. When your vision of success becomes greater than your fear of falling short, your harvest of success will completely overshadow your misfortunes. Year after year, Tom Brady makes fearless throws on game-winning drives to lead his team to victory. What if he allowed a mistake of his past to prevent him from making the big-time decisions when the game is on the line? What if he decides to play it safe by only making mediocre plays that minimize his chances of failure? What if those hungry lions were overwhelmed with the possibility of being outmatched by the elephant? Luckily for the New England Patriots, Brady doesn't allow the thought of failure to affect his play. Because he approaches each opportunity with a tunnel vision of success, he will go down as one the best and most fearless quarterbacks to ever play in the NFL. Former Cowboy running back, Phillip Tanner, says "Brady is so good because of his preparation. Preparation and confidence are everything. The work he puts in before he steps out on the field makes game day a piece of cake." With five Super Bowl rings to his name, success has become a part of Brady's nature and the fear of failure is unknown to him.

Here's a challenge to rid yourself of all distractions at this very moment. Take a moment to silence your cell phone and put it out of arm's reach. Take the next few seconds to cut your television off or mute any audio in order to make the room silent. If you happen to be eating, let your mouth rest for the next few moments. Taking notes is not permissible right now, so drop your pen. If you are taking on any form of multi-tasking, now is the time to stop. Think for a moment about how often this takes place during your week. For most of us, mental solitude is a rare occasion with our fast-paced society forcing us to make fools of ourselves by attempting to tackle multiple tasks at a time. Now that you have taken the time to free yourself from the responsibilities of your life, take your mind to your place of peace. Think about that place that is relaxing and relieving for you. It doesn't matter if your mind goes to a place of natural serenity that encompasses the peaceful flight of butterflies and the sweet aroma of your favorite flower; or to the comfort of lying in your bed staring at the ceiling as you gather thoughts for the upcoming day. What's important is that you envision yourself in this peaceful place. Now picture yourself making plans to accomplish your biggest goal. What is that one idea or concept that you want to prosper more than anything else? Picture yourself making strides toward making that dream come true. Think about all of the steps you have to make to get your business started, the money you have saved, and the books you have read. Ponder all the hours you have put in towards perfecting your craft and preparing yourself for opportunities. Now here's the fun part. Imagine when the opportunity you have wanted actually presents itself. Think about how you will present your business proposal, win your first court case, or run your first marathon. Whatever the opportunity is, mentally grasp it and make it as real as possible in your head by envisioning how you will make eye contact with investors, how you will follow through on every throw, or how you will engage the audience while on stage. Again, regardless of how it will take place for you, allow the thought to fill your imagination. To wrap up this thought process, I want you to imagine being told no. Maybe it's investors saying no to your business proposal or a record label saying no to your album. Maybe you are denied entrance into medical school or the chance to purchase your first home. Despite the way it happens to you, rejection always hurts and leaves its mark. Nobody enjoys being rejected or denied an opportunity. As prideful as we have grown in our world, rejection is the common reminder of humility. The pain of rejection often reproduces itself as *fear of rejection*. This fear looms so greatly because it involves the affirmation of people. At different points in our lives, we have all sought affirmation that gives us confidence and relevance. When it comes to our goals and dreams, we continuously seek affirmation because we want to invite others into our passion. As you grow closer to your life's goals, affirmation comes in the form of receiving the positive nods that can help you get to your desired end. It is often this affirmation that lays one step away from major accomplishment. This is when you have exhausted yourself of all your efforts and have placed your hope in others to culminate your journey. When I completed my senior year of college football, I worked tirelessly to give my best showing to NFL teams on my pro day. The hours of training I put in are beyond estimation and there is not much I would change about that three-month journey. When the day came for me to perform, I felt confident that I would get a chance at playing on some level of professional football. That chance never came and ultimately, I felt rejection. I had done everything in my power to prepare and those coaches were the affirmation I needed to reach my goal. The same happened with dozens of applications I submitted to jobs all over the nation. In both instances, it hurt. How has rejection happened to you? Can you remember that hurt? A more important question to ask yourself is, have you allowed that hurt to fester into a *fear of rejection*? Becoming a bystander of your own life's story is a fundamental mistake that can result from being rejected. Overcoming this mistake can only happen by understanding that what you have to offer the world cannot be rejected. You can be rejected in a number of ways by people, but your gifts, passions, and talents will pave a way in any wilderness of rejection. In other words, people can deny you, but they cannot deny your purpose. Some 20th century bakeries didn't like Otto Rohwedder for his idea to create sliced bread. However, regardless of ill feelings toward him, his idea was undeniable and is now seen as one of the best ideas known to man. Dedicate yourself to your purpose without fear of rejection. In fact, embrace rejection as a means to extract even better ideas from your innermost being. Remain intrigued by rejection and allow it to drive you to erase the reasons that people can deny you. Become your own biggest critic and filter, filter, filter! Evaluating your own work and ideas should allow you to create a checklist of why people could possibly reject you. It is your duty to eliminate those possibilities for rejection by continuously cycling through better ways to become a better you. Envisioning yourself as the decision-maker, pose the tough questions to yourself. By doing this, you liberate yourself from foreign encounters concerning your ideas, passions, and gifts. You will now be positioned with a confidence to seize opportunities instead of fearing reasons for rejection. How much do you really believe in yourself? Ask yourself how the world would be different with the knowledge of your presence. Can the world afford to reject you forever? After answering those questions, encourage yourself to overcome the fear of rejection by marrying yourself to your goals, dreams, and aspirations.

The word *change* often carries with it a negative connotation that quickly cripples people with fear because the word itself is a call to action. The word serves notice that alteration has or will occur. When pursuing purpose, *fear of change* can bring an abrupt halt to one's pursuit. This category of fear is not predicated on the satisfaction or dissatisfaction of others, but is a screaming challenge for you to *do something different.* *Fear of change* comes in countless forms. Maybe the comfort of a stable job is prohibiting you from creating your own business opportunities. Maybe the idea of leaving the city limits you're accustomed to will prevent you from taking the new job. Are you lost in a dead-end relationship because you have never envisioned yourself with someone else? Have you found yourself trapped by the responsibility of trying to uphold family traditions? Here's a note to tattoo on your heart: Change simply means to rearrange your priorities. Understand that priorities do not and should not remain the same throughout your lifetime. It is seemingly acceptable for every facet of our lives to change. Our ages change. Our homes change. Our relationships change. Everything around us seems to have an acceptable cycle of change, but we often forego changing our priorities.

The pressing issues of our life that drive us each day should not be identical year after year. These priorities may very well be similar or related; however; for these priorities to remain identical is a sign of stagnation. Change (rearranging priorities) should be an enjoyable sector of life. Rearranging priorities should always be pushing you closer to your passion. Categorizing your purpose as a minor priority is an injustice to yourself. This injustice is a byproduct of the fear to change. There are steps that must be taken in order to reach any goal of substance. Certainly, there are goals in life that you can stumble upon without making any significant changes to a particular way of life; however, the goals that you will truly value on your roadmap of life will often require you to embrace change. I often had conversations about change with my college roommate, Chris Collins. There were times we would cultivate each other's mind with questions about politics, religion, sports, and many other topics that ignite differing opinions. Innately, without intention, we were participating in a practice that is more commonly neglected now than ever before. The practice of allowing verbal, interpersonal communication to sharpen and build upon previous ideas has been lost in the shuffle of social media and other methods of communication. Many new-age avenues of communication do not promote impromptu and heartfelt dialogue. It was often in these conversations that both Chris and I realized something. An overwhelming majority of people are plagued by the *fear of change*. Chris went on to get his Master's degree in Health Promotion while also personal training at one of the largest gyms in the United States. I once sat down with Chris to ask about how the *fear of change* impacts him in his line of work as a personal trainer. Chris said, "It's just like change in any other area of life–uncertainty. People are hesitant to the unknown and are cool with the status quo, but in order to grow you have to be willing to take on something new and believe that it will work out." Chris caused me to truly meditate on a thought. When daring to make changes in life, believing in a better future is the only force that will prompt the boldness to act. There is a special corridor in everyone's heart where believing is conceived. From this special place comes a call to action. Both of my grandfathers died from cancer and I often questioned my father about where the power of cancer came from. Despite his expertise in the field of biology, he gave me a very simple answer. He informed me that cancer was so powerful because of the ability of cancer cells to reproduce faster than the human body could destroy them. Eventually, the reproduction of cancer cells damages the body in such a way that it is incapable of returning to its normal state of healthy existence. Believing works in a like manner. It only takes an ounce of belief to reproduce more and more belief. Before you know it, that special corridor can no longer contain the power of your belief and the *fear of change* becomes overtaken by a new confidence that continually reproduces itself. On the other end of that spectrum is doubt, and it reproduces in the same exponential pattern. Will you let doubt overtake you by magnifying the *fear of change*? Realize there is one person that can make the changes needed to fulfill your inspiration. Others can peek into your potential, but only you have the power to reach your potential.

Despite your inspiration, determination, and zeal, life presents an abundance of distractions that will hinder your progress. These are the moments when you have to fight for your focus. Climbing towards your destiny will not be an easy road. Because you're taking the road less traveled, there will be obstacles that you will have to learn to overcome on your own. There are certain battles you will have to learn strategic ways to win. The desire to go places people haven't gone requires the willingness to fight battles people haven't had to fight. Setting your eyes on your inspiration in these moments will give you a solid foundation. The truest form of success happens when people decide to create an original path to destiny. Learn from the journey of others, but travel a journey of your own. Stretch yourself beyond your wildest dream and chase the purpose of your heart with an unrivaled tenacity.

REFLECTION POINTS

Imagine this: List your 3 biggest obstacles that lie between you and your destiny.

Answer this: What journeys have fear prevented you from starting?

Try this: Remind yourself that you are your biggest barrier. Decide on one goal you want to start pursuing today.

www.ingramcontent.com/pod-product-compliance
Lightning Source LLC
Chambersburg PA
CBHW070505100426
42743CB00010B/1763